Activities to Undo Math Misconceptions

PreK–Grade 2

Activities to Undo Math Misconceptions

PreK–Grade 2

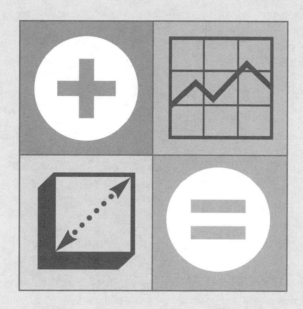

Honi J. Bamberger
Karren Schultz-Ferrell

HEINEMANN ✖ Portsmouth, NH

Heinemann

361 Hanover Street

Portsmouth, NH 03801–3912

www.heinemann.com

Offices and agents throughout the world

The authors and publisher wish to thank those who have generously given permission to reprint borrowed material:

"Pentomino Arrangements" from *Introduction to Reasoning and Proof: Grades 3–5* by Karren Schultz-Ferrell, Brenda Hammond, and Josepha Robles. Copyright © 2007 by Karren Schultz-Ferrell, Brenda Hammond, and Josepha Robles. Published by Heinemann. Reprinted by permission of the publisher.

Library of Congress Cataloging-in-Publication Data

Bamberger, Honi Joyce.
  Activities to undo math misconceptions : preK–grade 2 / Honi J. Bamberger, Karren Schultz-Ferrell.
    p. cm.
  ISBN-13: 978-0-325-02614-5
  ISBN-10: 0-325-02614-9
1. Mathematics—Study and teaching (Preschool)—United States—Activity programs. 2. Mathematics—Study and teaching (Primary)—United States—Activity programs. 3. Mathematics—Study and teaching (Preschool)—United States.
4. Mathematics—Study and teaching (Primary)—United States. I. Schultz-Ferrell, Karren. II. Bamberger, Honi Joyce. Math misconceptions. III. Title.
  QA135.6 .B366 2010 Suppl. 1
  372.7—dc22
                                                    2010016302

Editor: Victoria Merecki
Production: Sonja S. Chapman & Elizabeth Valway
Cover design: Night & Day Design
Interior design: Jenny Jensen Greenleaf
Composition: Publishers' Design and Production Services, Inc.
Manufacturing: Steve Bernier

Printed in the United States of America on acid-free paper
14 13 12 11 10 VP 1 2 3 4 5

Contents

Measurement 85

Data Analysis and Probability 107

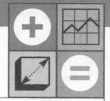

Acknowledgments

Writing books takes a discipline that goes above and beyond the call of duty, especially as we've juggled full-time jobs. We'd like to thank all of the editors at Heinemann whose assistance and patience allowed us to take the time we needed to "get it right." We also appreciate the sacrifices that our families (husbands, children, and even grandchildren) have made as we've taken time away from them to complete these books. Thank you, too, to Govans Elementary and to Oak View Elementary for allowing us to photograph children and activities for the books and for supporting us as we worked on them. Finally, a special thanks to the educators who inspire us and remind us to continue to learn as much as we can so we can inspire them.

Introduction

As experienced teachers who now spend our time working with both preservice and inservice teachers, we have talked at length about the challenges that students have with specific math content. Year after year, in one faculty room or another, teachers discuss first graders who still don't know how to count, third graders who still don't know how to add, and fifth graders who have no idea what a fraction is. How is it that no matter where we go there are second graders who don't "get" subtraction with renaming? And, why is it that fourth-grade students don't realize that a square is a special kind of rectangle? And, how is it possible that children in Alabama, New Jersey, Colorado, Pennsylvania, and Maryland (all places where we have worked) forget to say "fifteen" when they are counting by rote, by ones?

There had to be reasons why we kept seeing the same errors and misconceptions across states, in lots of classrooms, by many different students. So, nearly two years ago we began talking with teachers about the most common mistakes their students were making. We examined how relevant concepts and skills were taught, and we reviewed the mathematics programs that were being used. We found that, despite their best intentions, teachers often inadvertently contributed to the problems students were having. Early childhood educators, in their desire to nurture, support, and encourage young learners, could often be heard telling children, "Remember to always subtract the smaller number from the larger number." Or, when a student identifies a rhombus by calling it a "diamond," the teacher may tell the student what a good job he is doing with his shapes. As a result, students may not be learning the correct terminology of shapes or distinguishing numerals from digits. Young children don't really distinguish between digits, numerals, and numbers, so a first grader and second grader may think, when seeing 41 – 27, that the "1" should be subtracted from the "7" because it's the smaller of the "numbers." So, in an effort to make a difficult procedure easier a teacher may say something that could contribute to a misconception that is difficult to change.

It certainly isn't just the things that educators say or don't say that can cause misconceptions. One need only look at the numerous posters and resource materials that can be bought for the early childhood and elementary classroom to see that there are many errors in these.

Let's take a look at posters, math-related literature, and resource books on geometry. Without naming names we frequently see "diamond" as the label for a rhombus, "oval" as the label for an ellipse, and "t-shaped polygons" (dodecagons) being called "crosses." We are even more concerned by the teacher resource materials and posters that provide students with "key words" to remember in order to solve addition, subtraction, multiplication, and division word problems. Posters may have the operation listed and then beneath it key words that students should be looking for so they know what to do to solve specific problems. Some curricula even have entire lessons written that tell teachers how to introduce and reinforce these "key words."

What makes this so bad? If the purpose of mathematics instruction is to teach for understanding, then looking for words and numerals, rather than the meaning behind the story, negates that purpose. And, since when does *altogether* only mean "add"? This story, "Altogether there are 23 children playing on the playground. Nine are girls and the rest are boys. How many boys are on the playground?" does not have students adding to find the answer.

◻ About This Book

Armed with resource books, posters, curricula, and statements made by well-meaning teachers, we looked at the error patterns and misconceptions that we were seeing in classroom after classroom. In this book, we address the most common errors we found in each of the five National Council of Teachers of Mathematics (NCTM) content strands: number and operations, algebra, geometry, measurement, and data analysis and probability. We offer you numerous instructional ideas for remediating a particular error, or for preventing a misconception from ever taking root. We also include black-line masters for nearly thirty activities and games that you can immediately incorporate into your classroom instruction. For each misconception, we also offer "Look Fors" to help guide your formative assessment during independent or small-group work. Finally, the accompanying CD-ROM includes editable versions of all of the black-line masters found in these pages. This allows you to customize our activities, either by differentiating the level of difficulty or making the situations more relevant to your particular students.

◻ An Additional Resource

This activity book is a companion to our comprehensive resource book, *Math Misconceptions, PreK–Grade 5: From Misunderstanding to Deep Understanding*. In the resource book we share classroom vignettes and problem-based situations that give you additional insight into the misconception or error pattern that is being described. We also highlight relevant research and offer a range of instructional suggestions.

Our hope is that you will first read the resource book for a comprehensive discussion of the range of student misconceptions and the reasons behind them. You can then use this activity book to save yourself time in preparing some of the instructional ideas we discuss. However, if you choose to use only this activity book you will still gain useful insight into some of the more common mathematics errors and misconceptions and numerous ideas for addressing them.

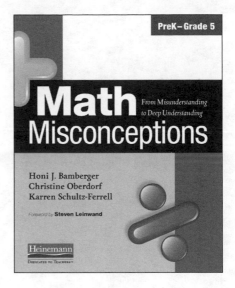

Counting

 Misconception

Creating a student-generated pattern in the counting sequence to make sense of the existing sequence. For example, students recite one through ten correctly, but then continue, "one-teen, two-teen, three-teen, four-teen, five-teen…nineteen" or "tenty-one, tenty-two, tenty-three…"

What to Do

- Read counting books and then make them available to students in a center area (see page 2).

- Count together out loud. Students count higher when counting together and will hear the sequence modeled correctly. Count backward as well. Allow certain students to count independently so number sounds are clear.

- Provide opportunities for students to recite counting rhymes.

- Prepare cards with each showing a numeral and a set that represents that numeral.

- Provide salad tongs so students can pick up each item as it is counted, or give them a pointer stick so they can point to each item as it is counted.

- Provide egg cartons or ice cube trays for counting out items, placing each item in a space.

- Let students play path games (see page 4).

- Model how to keep track using a work mat with a line drawn down the middle. Students move objects one at a time across the line as they count objects. Let students count objects, taken one at a time from a bag, and place them on a mat.

- Ask "How many?" each time a student finishes counting to reinforce cardinality. Or when counting together say, "1, 2, 3, 4, 5, 6. We have 6 cubes."

- Begin counting by ones from numbers other than "one."

- Ask students to count while in a circle. Choose a designated number such as 12. When any student counts "12," he sits down. Continue counting around the circle.

- Allow students to make a train of dominoes by placing a domino with one more on each turn. They justify its placement by saying, "6 comes after 5."

Look Fors

As students work through these activities, check for the following understandings:

✔ How far can students count in a stable-order count?

✔ How high can a student count using one-to-one correspondence?

✔ What strategy does the student use for keeping track?

✔ Through what number does the student have cardinality?

Counting

Bibliography

This recommended list of engaging and interactive books helps young children strengthen their counting skills. A brief description details the counting being reinforced.

Andreason, Dan. 2007. *The Baker's Dozen: A Counting Book*. New York: Henry Holt. (Counting up to 12)

Anno, Mitsumasa. 1992. *Anno's Counting Book (Big Book)*. New York: Harper Trophy. (Counting up to 12)

Barrett, Judi. 2000. *I Knew Two Who Said Moo*. New York: Atheneum Books for Young Readers. (Counting up to 10 and rhyming everyday words to number words)

Coxe, Molly. 1999. *6 Sticks*. New York: Random House. (Counting up to 6; after reading, let students create different representations of 6 craft sticks)

Dugan, Joanne. 2007. *123NYC: A Counting Book of New York City*. New York: Abrams Books for Young Readers. (Counting 1–20)

Ehlert, Lois. 1992. *Fish Eyes: A Book You Can Count On*. New York: Voyager Books. (Counting up to 10; on final pages students count 22 fish eyes)

Gerth, Melanie. 2000. *Ten Little Ladybugs*. Santa Monica, CA: Piggy Toes Press. (Counting backward from 10)

Giganti, Paul. 1994. *How Many Snails? A Counting Book*. New York: Harper Trophy. (Counting a variety of groupings)

Micklethwait, Lucy. 1993. *I Spy Two Eyes: Numbers in Art*. New York: Mulberry Books. (Counting objects from 1–20 in famous art works)

Murphy, Chuck. 1995. *One to Ten: Pop-Up Surprises!* New York: Simon & Schuster. (Counting up to 10; engaging illustrations)

Murphy, Stuart J. 1997. *Every Buddy Counts*. New York: Harper Collins. (Numerals and number words up to 10)

O'Leary, John. 1995. *Ten on a Train*. New York: Puffin Books. (Counting backward from 10)

Paparone, Pamela (Illustrator). 1995. *Five Little Ducks*. New York: North-South Books, Inc. (Counting backward from 5)

Rose, Deborah Lee. 2003. *The Twelve Days of Kindergarten: A Counting Book*. New York: Harry N. Abrams. (Counting up to 12 using numerals and ordinal numbers)

Wahl, John, and Stacey Wahl. 1999. *I Can Count the Petals of a Flower*. Reston, VA: National Council of Teachers of Mathematics. (Counting up to 10 and 16. Counting in other languages included)

Walsh, Ellen Stoll. 1991. *Mouse Count*. New York: Voyager Books. (Counting forward and backward from ten)

Wells, Rosemary. 2000. *Emily's First 100 Days of Schools*. New York: Hyperion Books for Children. (Counting 1–100 with connections to everyday life)

Back and Forth

In this path game, students reinforce oral counting, one-to-one correspondence, and cardinality through 6.

Materials
- Back and Forth game board (see page 5) (one per pair of students)
- Counters (one per pair of students)
- Dot cubes (one cube per pair of students)
- Cups (or detergent lids) to "shake and spill" number cube (one per pair of students)

■ First model the game by asking student to take turns playing a game with you.

■ The counter is placed in the center circle on the game board. This counter is shared by both partners.

■ Partners decide which "home" circle will be theirs: Player 1 or Player 2.

■ The first partner shakes the number cube three times and spills onto the game board. She identifies or counts the resulting number and moves the counter that many spaces toward her home circle.

■ The other partner then takes his turn, shaking and spilling the number cube. He moves the same counter the correct number of spaces from where it is on the game board. However, he moves the counter in the direction of his home circle.

■ The counter moves back and forth until it eventually reaches one of the home circles.

Ideas for Differentiation

■ Students use a cube with the numerals 1 through 6.

■ Students use an alternate cube. This can be made by placing small sticky dots on each face of a cube and recording numerals 1, 2, and 3 twice; or, for students needing greater numerals, 5 through 10.

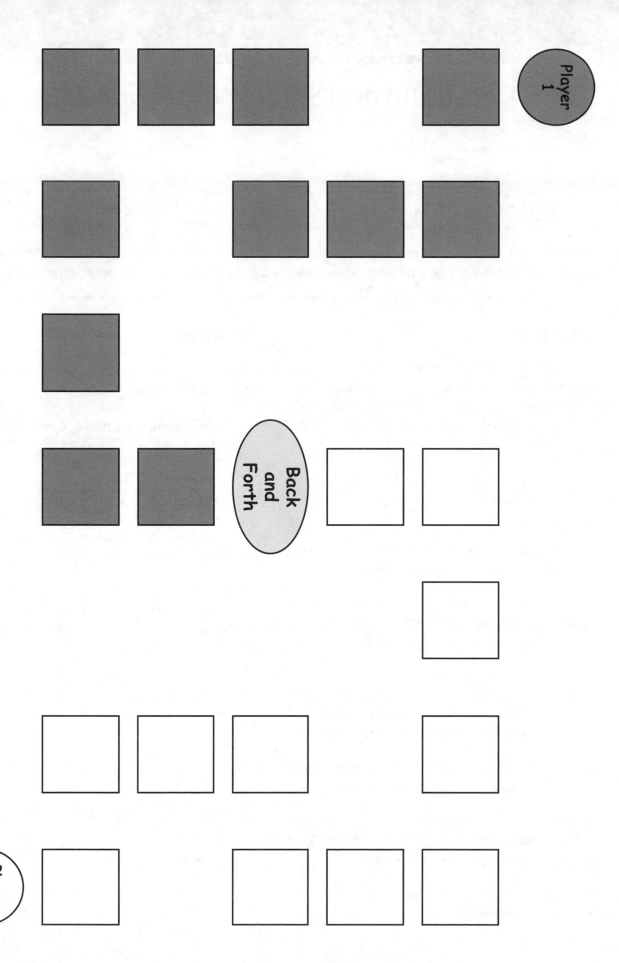

Addition and Subtraction Concepts

Misconception

Thinking that addition always means "put together" or "join" and subtraction always means "take away" or "separate," making it difficult for students to solve a variety of addition and subtraction problem types.

What to Do

■ Before using symbols, provide students with a variety of materials that can be used to create part-whole representations of numbers (bicolored counters, connecting cubes, teddy bear counters, Cuisenaire® Rods).

■ Use correct terminology for the addition and subtraction signs (+ plus) and (– minus).

■ Provide students with opportunities to solve story problems that include all four problem types: join, separate, part-part-total, and compare.

■ Provide students with some manipulative material to model the story problem that's been given; but have them also symbolically record what they've done.

■ During a discussion about solutions to story problems, ask students to share the strategies they used to get their answers, reinforcing correct terminology.

■ Use dominoes to have students generate part-whole addition number sentences.

■ Use classroom routines to generate meaningful comparative subtraction problem solving. A "YES/NO" graph will provide daily comparisons.

■ Provide students with opportunities to develop their own story problems.

Look Fors

As students work through these activities, check for the following understandings:

✔ When students share their equations, listen for the correct use of "minus" and "plus."

✔ When students solve comparison subtraction story problems, look to see if students create two sets. Then look to see if they use an appropriate strategy to determine how many more or fewer one set is compared to the other.

✔ When students generate their own stories, look to see if they are developing a variety of problems based on the types and structures taught.

Name _____ Date _____

Using Dominoes to Solve Story Problems

There are 8 pips altogether.
Show two different ways to represent this.

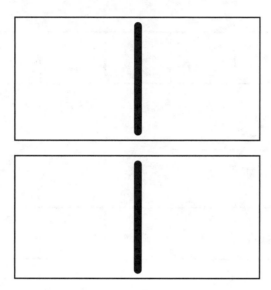

There are 6 pips altogether.
Show two different ways to represent this.

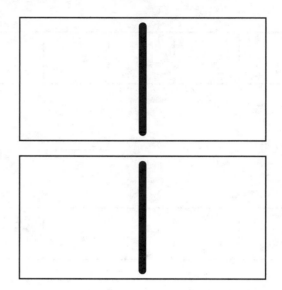

There are 5 pips altogether.
Show two different ways to represent this.

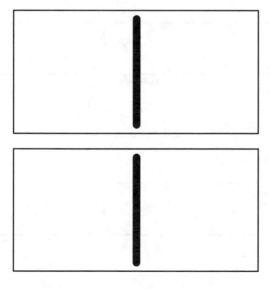

There are 10 pips altogether.
Show two different ways to represent this.

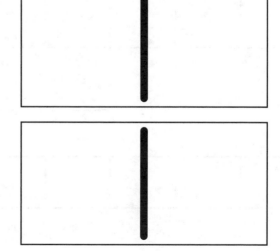

Using Connecting Cubes to Show Addition Equations

Take two different colors of cubes. Show different ways to make 10. Color the strip and write the equation.

_____ + _____ = _____

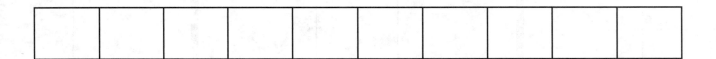

_____ + _____ = _____

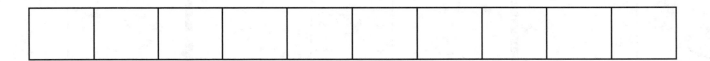

_____ + _____ = _____

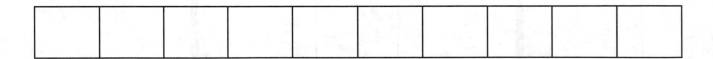

_____ + _____ = _____

Number and Operations: *Addition and Subtraction Concepts*

Name _____ Date _____

Story Problems to Solve

Read each story.
Solve each story with counters, pictures, or symbols.
Write the number sentence to match each story.

Johnny has 9 toy trucks.

Susie has 4 toy trucks.

How many more trucks does Johnny have?

Number sentence: _____

Brandi is reading her library book.

So far she has read 5 pages.

There are 12 pages in the whole book.

How many more pages does she need to read?

Number sentence: _____

In her candy bag Pat has 15 candies.

8 of them are chocolate.

The others are vanilla.

How many vanilla candies does Pat have?

Number sentence: _____

Name _____ Date _____

Spinning for a Sum

See Appendix A for the spinners to be used with this activity.

Place a paper clip in the center of each spinner. Spin and record the addends. Use counters to help you figure out the sum.

First Problem Spun	Second Problem Spun
_____ + _____ = _____	_____ + _____ = _____
Third Problem Spun	Fourth Problem Spun
_____ + _____ = _____	_____ + _____ = _____
Fifth Problem Spun	Sixth Problem Spun
_____ + _____ = _____	_____ + _____ = _____
Seventh Problem Spun	Eighth Problem Spun
_____ + _____ = _____	_____ + _____ = _____

Name _____ Date _____

Using a Graph to Add and Subtract

Number of Letters in Our First Names

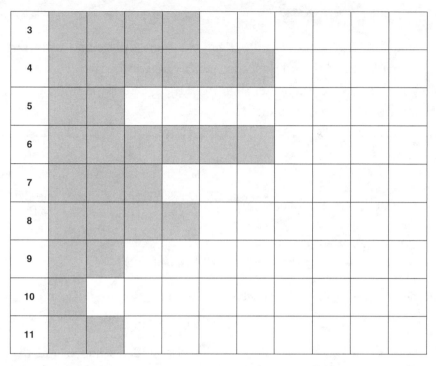

Use the data from the graph to represent addition and subtraction equations. Figure out the answers to each problem.

■ How many more people have 6 letters than 5 letters?

_____

■ How many people have 8 or 9 letters in their name?

_____

■ How many more people have 4 letters than 7 letters?

_____

■ How many people have 6 or 4 letters in their name?

_____

Place Value: Addition and Subtraction of Two-Digit Numerals

 Misconception

When adding two-digit numbers begin with the digits in the ones place and record the entire sum; then add the digits in the tens place and record this sum. When subtracting two-digit numbers begin with the digits in the ones place and subtract the lesser digit from the greater digit; then go to the tens place and subtract the lesser digit from the greater digit.

What to Do

- Have students use their understanding of counting by ones to group larger quantities, making it easier to count (grouping by twos, fives, or tens).

- Have students use a hundreds chart to look for patterns, and determine simple sums and differences by moving around the chart (34 + 2 = ; 46 – 3 = ; 18 + 4 = ; 41 – 3 =).

- Use estimation activities so students get regular practice estimating quantities and then determining the actual amount by grouping by tens.

- Have students share their solutions and the strategies that they used to get their answers. This allows all students to see that there is more than one way to compute to find a sum or difference.

- Play games that require students to bundle, connect, or place objects together when there are ten of the object. Have students then record the quantity of tens and ones and the number that this represents.

- Give students a two-digit number and have them represent, either through modeling, pictures, or symbols, all of the ways to show this number using tens and ones only.

- Finally, have students use whatever strategy is *efficient* and *effective* in getting a sum or difference as long as it makes sense to them.

Look Fors

As students work through these activities, check for the following understandings:

✔ Do students understand the value of each digit rather than looking at the digit in isolation?

✔ Are students able to compose and decompose numbers?

✔ Do students see addition and subtraction as inverse operations?

Name _____ Date _____

A Bake Sale at Walt Whitman Elementary School

You may use any materials to help you solve each story problem. Once the problem has been solved, represent your strategy on this paper. You may use drawings, symbols, or words to show your answer and what you did to get your answer.

Story 1: Janet and her dad baked cookies for the class bake sale. On Saturday morning they baked 2 dozen cookies. In the afternoon, they baked 3 dozen cookies. How many cookies will Janet bring to the bake sale?

Story 2: Marquis is bringing 38 chocolate-iced cupcakes to the bake sale. Ronald is bringing 25 vanilla-iced cupcakes to the bake sale. How many more cupcakes is Marquis bringing?

Story 3: Lydia and Kathie cut the pan of brownies that they baked into 40 brownies. Germaine made brownies, too. In his pan there are 32 brownies. How many brownies will there be at the class bake sale?

Story 4: Brenda and her mom made caramel popcorn balls to sell at the bake sale. They made 54 balls and wrapped them in waxed paper. When she was putting these into her sack to bring to school Brenda counted only 48 caramel popcorn balls. Her sister and brother ate some. How many did they eat?

Name _____ Date _____

Make 100

Toss 2 numeral cubes and say the sum. Take this many connecting cubes and place them on your mat. When you have enough single cubes to make a stick of 10, place your 10 stick on the left side of your mat. Leave your single ones on the right side of your mat. Record what happens during your turn.

1st turn: I tossed a _____ and a _____. This equals _____. On my mat I have

_____ tens and _____ ones. This is the number _____.

2nd turn: I tossed a _____ and a _____. This equals _____. Now on my mat I

have _____ tens and _____ ones. This is the number _____.

3rd turn: I tossed a _____ and a _____. This equals _____. Now on my mat I

have _____ tens and _____ ones. This is the number _____.

4th turn: I tossed a _____ and a _____. This equals _____. Now on my mat I

have _____ tens and _____ ones. This is the number _____.

5th turn: I tossed a _____ and a _____. This equals _____. Now on my mat I

have _____ tens and _____ ones. This is the number _____.

6th turn: I tossed a _____ and a _____. This equals _____. Now on my mat I

have _____ tens and _____ ones. This is the number _____.

7th turn: I tossed a _____ and a _____. This equals _____. Now on my mat I

have _____ tens and _____ ones. This is the number _____.

Number and Operations: *Place Value: Addition and Subtraction of Two-Digit Numerals*

8th turn: I tossed a _____ and a _____. This equals _____. Now on my mat I have _____ tens and _____ ones. This is the number _____.

9th turn: I tossed a _____ and a _____. This equals _____. Now on my mat I have _____ tens and _____ ones. This is the number _____.

10th turn: I tossed a _____ and a _____. This equals _____. Now on my mat I have _____ tens and _____ ones. This is the number _____.

11th turn: I tossed a _____ and a _____ This equals _____. Now on my mat I have _____ tens and _____ ones. This is the number _____.

12th turn: I tossed a _____ and a _____. This equals _____. Now on my mat I have _____ tens and _____ ones. This is the number _____.

I ended this game with a total of _____ cubes. I had _____ sticks of ten and _____ single ones. I needed _____ single cubes more to make 100. I could also have shown this as _____ tens sticks and _____ ones.

Number and Operations: *Place Value: Addition and Subtraction of Two-Digit Numerals*

Name _____ Date _____

Get to ZERO

Begin this game with 9 sticks of 10 on your mat. Then toss 2 numeral cubes and say the sum. This amount needs to be taken off your mat. (HINT: You may need to break apart a stick of 10 to get single cubes to take off.) Record what you've done on this sheet.

I started with _____ tens. I had to take off _____.
Now I have _____ tens and _____ ones; or the number _____.

For my 2nd turn I started with _____. I had to take off _____. I'm left with _____ tens and _____ ones; or the number _____.

For my 3rd turn I started with _____. I had to take off _____. I'm left with _____ tens and _____ ones; or the number _____.

For my 4th turn I started with _____. I had to take off _____. I'm left with _____ tens and _____ ones; or the number _____.

For my 5th turn I started with _____. I had to take off _____. I'm left with _____ tens and _____ ones; or the number _____.

For my 6th turn I started with _____. I had to take off _____. I'm left with _____ tens and _____ ones; or the number _____.

For my 7th turn I started with _____. I had to take off _____. I'm left with _____ tens and _____ ones; or the number _____.

For my 8th turn I started with _____. I had to take off _____. I'm left with _____ tens and _____ ones; or the number _____.

For my 9th turn I started with _____. I had to take off _____. I'm left with _____ tens and _____ ones; or the number _____.

For my 10th turn I started with _____. I had to take off _____. I'm left with _____ tens and _____ ones; or the number _____.

My final number is _____. This is _____ away from zero.

Number and Operations: *Place Value: Addition and Subtraction of Two-Digit Numerals*

Foundational Ideas for Multiplication and Division

⊕ Misconception

Applying addition and subtraction strategies erroneously to multiplication and division situations. For example, when multiplying 9×3 students round 9 to 10, calculate 10×3, and then subtract a single value of 1 to accommodate for the rounding, rather than 3 groups of 1.

What to Do

- Number Lines

  Rulers, yardsticks, and meter sticks can serve as number lines to model multiplication and division situations (see page 18).

- Equal Groupings

  Making equal groups to model multiplication allows students to create equal sets and reinforces the notion that all sets are the same size (see page 19). For the problem 9×3, when rounding 9 to 10 and then multiplying by 3, the students must understand that the readjustment of subtracting 1 applies to each of the 3 groups.

- Partial Products

  The partial products strategy emphasizes the importance of place value when multiplying whole numbers and provides an alternative algorithm that emphasizes the whole number rather than isolated digits within a number.

  Partial Products:

  $$\begin{array}{l} 12 \text{ equals } 10 \text{ plus } 2 \\ \underline{\times 6} \qquad \underline{\times 6} \quad \underline{\times 6} \\ \qquad \quad 60 \ + 12 = 72 \end{array}$$

The same can be done by pulling out equal groups for division and then finding the total quotient by adding all of the partials.

Partial Quotients:

$$\begin{array}{l} 6 \overline{)72} \qquad 6 \times \mathbf{10} = 60 \\ \quad \underline{-60} \qquad 6 \times \mathbf{2} = 12 \\ \qquad 12 \qquad 10 + 2 = \mathbf{12} \end{array}$$

- Area Model of Multiplication

  By using an area model in conjunction with a rounding strategy, students see the value of the rounded product and how it compares to the actual product. This representation displays why an adjustment is necessary and how much of an adjustment should be made to the rounded product.

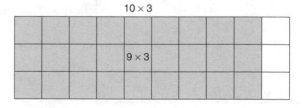

Look For

As students work through these activities, check for the following understanding:

- ✔ Do students understand that all groups must be the same size when solving multiplication and division problems?

Number Lines

Use the tools listed on the chart below to model multiplication and division on the number lines. Record the results in the columns below along with a sketch of your moves. See the example provided.

Tools	Description	Results
Example: 12-inch ruler, counter	**Show 3 hops of 3 inches each.**	*I moved 9 inches total.*
Yardstick, pipe cleaners	Display the number of 3-inch hops (multiples of 3) you must make to reach the end of the yardstick (36 inches). Make each hop with a pipe cleaner.	
Meter stick, pipe cleaners	Divide the meter stick into 4 equal parts. Mark each section with a pipe cleaner.	
You choose:	You describe:	

Number and Operations: *Foundational Ideas for Multiplication and Division*

Name _____ Date _____

Equal Groupings

See Appendix B for the spinner to be used with this activity.

Spin the spinner and toss a 1–6 number cube. The spinner tells you the size of each group, and the cube tells you the number of groups. Draw a picture of the multiplication problem and show the strategy you used to solve the equation.

What if you only needed to give an estimate for your turn? What would your estimate be and why?

Equal Groupings 2

Solve the problems below. Use words, pictures, or symbols to explain your answer.

Aaron has to make 8 prize bags for the community picnic. He has 32 trinkets. How many trinkets will Aaron put in each bag so all the bags have the same amount of trinkets?

What if Aaron needed to make 16 bags? How would this change the number of trinkets in each bag? Why?

Number and Operations: *Foundational Ideas for Multiplication and Division*

Foundational Ideas for Division

 ## Misconception

Not understanding the concept of division as repeated subtraction or recognizing division as the inverse operation of multiplication.

What to Do

- Before using symbols, provide students with a story problem that is meaningful to them.

- Provide students with some manipulative material to model the story that's been given, but also have them symbolically record what they've done.

- During a discussion ask students to share the strategies they used to get their answers and then discuss whether these answers make sense.

- "Try out" someone's procedure that is both efficient and effective to see if students are able to use this to solve division expressions.

- Use number sense activities to foster mental computation and an understanding of how to use multiples of ten to arrive at answers.

- Look at ways to adjust numbers to make them easier to use for computing.

Look Fors

As students work through these activities, check for the following understandings:

- ✔ Check to see if students have a procedure that will always work.

- ✔ As students use their own division algorithm make sure that they can articulate why it works and how they know their answer makes sense.

Story Problems to Solve

Use any strategy that works for you to solve the following story problems. Use words, pictures, or symbols to represent your answer.

Story Problem	Work to Solve It
Sheri is sharing her bag of candy with 2 of her friends. She's getting some candy, too. When she counted the candies she found out that there were 53. How many candies will each person get? If there are any leftover candies, what will Sheri do with them?	
Martin bought 60 inches of fabric to make scarves for his friends. Each scarf needs 15 inches of fabric. How many scarves will Martin get to make? Will there be any fabric left over?	
Maritza cut a piece of bulletin board paper to use for 2 bulletin boards in the classroom. Her piece of paper is 130 inches long. If each bulletin board gets the same amount of paper, how much paper will each board get?	

Number and Operations: *Foundational Ideas for Division*

Name _____   Date _____

Modeling Division

Sometimes you just need to practice dividing to get better at it. Use counters to show how you would find the answer to each of these problems. Then write the answer.

17 ÷ 3 =	23 ÷ 6 =
19 ÷ 4 =	27 ÷ 5 =
29 ÷ 8 =	20 ÷ 7 =

Division Puzzlers

Use what you know about division and what you know about real-life things to help you figure out the answers to each puzzler. Show the work you did to get each answer.

Cameron counted 48 legs on the dogs in the room. How many dogs were there?

Taking a handful of hexagons, David counted 54 angles. How many hexagons did he take?

Crawling across the floor were the legs of lots of spiders. Nikki counted 48 legs. How many spiders were there?

Number and Operations: *Foundational Ideas for Division*

Fractions

 Misconception

Overgeneralizing the meaning of fractions due to limited experiences with dividing regions and sets into fair shares. For example, students identify one-half as one of two parts, rather than one of two equal parts.

What to Do

- Provide students multiple opportunities to share various objects that support them in thinking more flexibly about fractions. Present nontraditional shapes (such as a triangle) for students to divide (see page 26).

- Involve students in discussions following their work with fractions. Introduce fraction vocabulary and talk about fractional parts rather than fraction symbolism.

- Encourage students to "fair share" a grid outline in different ways (see page 27). For example, on a 4 × 4 grid of squares, the grid can be divided into halves by drawing a line through the middle either horizontally or vertically; the number of boxes (16) can also be divided into 2 areas of 8 in several ways.

- Provide opportunities for students to solve word problems involving both area and set models of fractions (see page 28).

- Provide students with opportunities to develop understandings about fractional concepts in a variety of real-life connections. Reach beyond the "pizza" connection!

- Present sharing problems that include the "set" model of fractions to help students establish important connections with many real-world uses of fractions.

- Provide opportunities for students to explore fractions such as eighths. Their understandings about "halving" can help them to work with a variety of fractions.

- Count fractional parts with students so they see how multiple parts compare to the whole (for example, one-fourth, two-fourths, three-fourths, four-fourths).

Look Fors

As students work through these activities, check for the following understandings:

✔ Are students able to fairly share an area in different ways?

✔ Are students able to divide a variety of shapes or objects accurately?

✔ Are students able to represent fractional parts in a variety of nontraditional or irregular shapes?

Fair Shares or Equal Parts

Color half of the circle red.
Color half of the triangle yellow.
Color half of the square blue.
Color half of the trapezoid black.

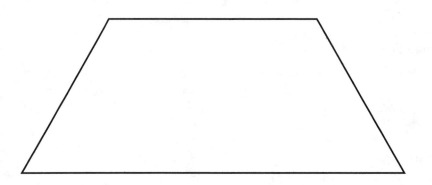
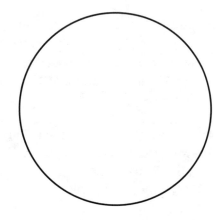
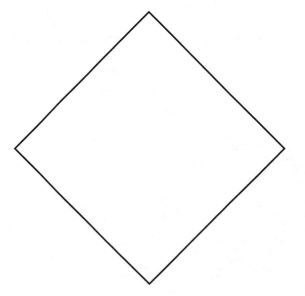
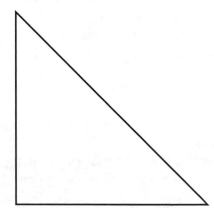

Name _____ Date _____

Fair Shares

Two sisters are sharing a pan of brownies. They will each take one-half of the brownies to a school party. How many different ways can you divide the pan of brownies into halves? Show your work on the grids below.

Sharing Word Problems

You have 5 candy bars. You want to share them with 3 friends.

Show how the candy bars can be shared so that you and your friends each have the same amount.

How can you share the candy bars so that you and 2 friends have the same amount?

You have 12 candies.

You want to share them with 3 friends.

Show how the candies can be shared so that you and your friends each have the same amount.

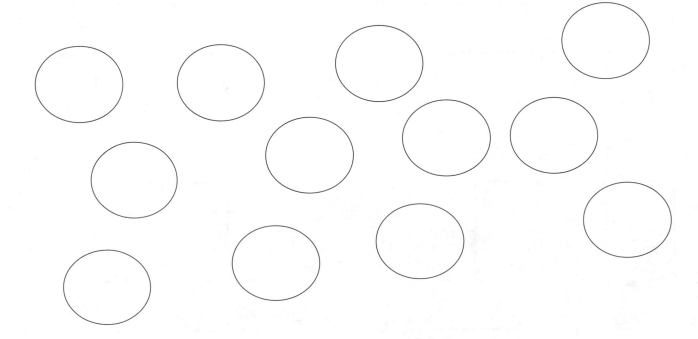

Number and Operations: *Fractions*

Foundational Ideas for Adding and Subtracting Fractions

Misconception

Applying procedures for addition and subtraction of whole numbers to addition and subtraction of fractions. For example, when adding common fractions with like denominators, students add the numerators together, and then add the denominators together. When subtracting common fractions with like denominators, students subtract the numerators, and then subtract the denominators.

What to Do

- Allow students to create their own materials or draw their own representations when adding and subtracting fractions.

- Introduce activities in which children count by fractions. Begin by using manipulatives with which children are already familiar—pattern blocks, for example.

- Have students combine their "fraction kits" (see page 30) so they can count by halves, thirds, fourths, sixths, eighths, and even twelfths. If they get good at this, ask them to combine strips from their kit: "If you have 5 of the one-twelfth pieces and you add 2 more one-twelfth pieces, what fraction will you have?" Be careful to ask the right questions. The answer to "How many pieces do you now have?" is 7, not the answer you want.

- Introduce story problems that reinforce what it means to add and subtract fractions. Don't have students record the equation until they have shared their strategies for getting their answers. Once students have been introduced to a number of examples ask, "What do you notice about how fractions are added or subtracted when the denominators are the same?" Reinforce that if you have eighths and add more eighths, you'll end up with even more eighths. It just makes sense.

- Use the number line to represent fractions. The number line is an effective tool for comparing the magnitude of fractions as well as adding and subtracting fractions with like denominators.

- Reveal patterns on the multiplication chart as an example of equivalent fractions. This exercise will serve as a precursor to students understanding how to name equivalent forms of a fractions when adding and subtracting fractions with unlike denominators.

Look Fors

As students work through these activities, check for the following understandings:

✔ The denominator names the total number of pieces needed to form the whole.

✔ The numerator indicates a specific number of pieces of the unit.

✔ While the numerator changes when adding and subtracting fractions with like denominators, the denominator remains the same in the sum or difference.

Making a Fraction Kit

You will need seven different colors of 9″ × 12″ construction paper. Students will need a 3″ × 12″ strip of the construction paper in all seven of the colors, as well as a 12″ ruler, scissors, crayons or markers, and a pencil. Once students have a strip of each of the seven colors, ask them which color will be used to represent one whole. Let the class decide, and then have students write "1" or "one" or "one-whole" on this piece. With each fraction ask students which color they want to represent the piece. In this way all of the kits will look the same. The kit will be made in this order: first the one-whole piece, then halves, fourths, eighths, thirds, sixths, and twelfths. Students can use clips to keep their fraction pieces together and store the kit in a gallon-sized bag. It is recommended that students record their initials on each piece to keep them from getting mixed up with other students' fraction kits.

When the color for halves has been decided, ask students how they think they'll need to fold the piece in order to get halves. Before they fold the paper, ask them these questions:

■ How many total pieces will you have when you've made halves?

■ What do you know about the pieces?

■ How do you represent the fraction one-half?

Then have them carefully fold the strip and write either "½" or "one-half" on each half.

Ask students to predict which fraction strip will be made next. It's likely that students will say, "thirds" since they are thinking in order of the denominators. When you tell them that fourths will be made next, ask them how knowing how to make halves might help them make fourths. Listen to their ideas and then give them these directions: "First fold your strip in half, the same way that you just made your halves. Now open each half so you can see the whole strip again. Fold one of your halves in half. Then fold the other half in half. Open your strip and see if you've made fourths." After each fraction is made, have students write the symbols and/or the word name on each piece. Then have students cut apart their parts.

Ask the same questions that you asked about halves for each of the fractions that will be folded, labeled, and cut. Have them predict the fraction that will be made next and then ask them how knowing how to fold fourths will help them fold eighths. When these have been made ask them very simple questions and have them use their pieces to get the answers:

- Which is greater, one-half or one-eighth?

- Which is less, one-fourth or one-half?

- How many fourths does it take to equal one-half?

- How many eighths does it take to equal one-half?

- How many eighths does it take to equal one-fourth?

- How many fourths does it take to equal one whole?

- One-fourth plus another one-fourth equals how many fourths?

For the next part of the fraction kit students will need to use their rulers. Emphasize the fact that fractional parts must be the same size, so estimating isn't such a good idea when making these. Have them talk with a partner about how using a ruler might help them make thirds (from their strip). Students might talk about dividing and suggest that since there are twelve inches in a foot-long ruler, and if there will be three pieces the same size, then each piece will need to be four inches in length. Have students use their rulers to create thirds, labeling them, and then cutting them.

At this point you might want to ask them questions about their halves, thirds, fourths, and eighths, or you may want to wait until the rest of the kit has been made. Ask students how knowing how to make thirds will help them to make sixths. They may decide to use the ruler and make two-inch pieces, or they may make thirds and then fold each third in half. Other strategies can be discussed. Have students make their sixths, and then make their twelfths.

This kit can be used for teaching equivalence, inequalities, counting by fractions, addition, subtraction, multiplication, and even division of fractions. And since students have made them it is likely that they will be able to state that the greater the denominator the more pieces there will be and the pieces will be smaller in size.

1 Whole							
$\frac{1}{2}$				$\frac{1}{2}$			
$\frac{1}{4}$		$\frac{1}{4}$		$\frac{1}{4}$		$\frac{1}{4}$	
$\frac{1}{8}$	$\frac{1}{8}$	$\frac{1}{8}$	$\frac{1}{8}$	$\frac{1}{8}$	$\frac{1}{8}$	$\frac{1}{8}$	$\frac{1}{8}$

$\frac{1}{3}$				$\frac{1}{3}$				$\frac{1}{3}$			
$\frac{1}{6}$		$\frac{1}{6}$		$\frac{1}{6}$		$\frac{1}{6}$		$\frac{1}{6}$		$\frac{1}{6}$	
$\frac{1}{12}$	$\frac{1}{12}$	$\frac{1}{12}$	$\frac{1}{12}$	$\frac{1}{12}$	$\frac{1}{12}$	$\frac{1}{12}$	$\frac{1}{12}$	$\frac{1}{12}$	$\frac{1}{12}$	$\frac{1}{12}$	$\frac{1}{12}$

Name _____   Date _____

Counting Fractions

Think of the yellow hexagon as one whole. Then count fractional parts using the red trapezoids, the blue rhombuses, and finally the green triangles. For example, with the red trapezoids you would count and label one-half, two-halves, three-halves, four-halves, and so on (see below). Repeat with the rhombuses and triangles. Once you have filled the page, trace around the shapes and record the fraction names for each.

One-half	Two-halves	Three-halves	Four-halves
$\frac{1}{2}$	$\frac{2}{2}$ or 1	$\frac{3}{2}$ or $1\frac{1}{2}$	$\frac{4}{2}$ or 2

Brownies for the Picnic

Read the story problem below. Use pictures, symbols, or words to solve this problem.

For the summer picnic, Mr. Phelps baked a pan of brownies that he cut into 8 equal-sized parts. Before he got to the picnic he noticed that $\frac{3}{8}$ of the pieces were missing. Mr. Phelps figured that his 3 children had each had a brownie. He thought that he should try them to make sure that they tasted good. Mr. Phelps ate another $\frac{2}{8}$ of the pan. What fractional part of the pan has already been eaten? What fractional part of the pan does he now have to bring to the picnic?

May be copied for classroom use. © 2010 by Honi J. Bamberger and Karren Schultz-Ferrell from *Activities to Undo Math Misconceptions, PreK–Grade 2* (Heinemann: Portsmouth, NH).

Number and Operations: *Foundational Ideas for Adding and Subtracting Fractions*

Foundational Ideas for Representing Decimals

 Misconception

Applying whole-number concepts to decimal fractions; for example, students order decimals by the number of digits rather than the value. Students also may align digits rather than decimal points when adding and subtracting decimals.

What to Do

- Correctly name the decimal fraction. When a decimal fraction is read correctly, the name reinforces the place value of each digit. Prevent students from getting into the habit of saying "six point three" rather than "six and three-tenths" when reading a decimal fraction.

- Use a variety of concrete models to represent decimal fractions. Students need multiple representations for decimal fractions. Such models include base-ten materials, money, meter sticks, and Digi-Blocks®.

- Provide opportunities to reinforce place value. With experience, students will recognize the relationship among adjacent values and see that moving to the left (by one digit) means *ten times larger*, and moving to the right denotes *one-tenth of the value*. Additionally, students must have opportunities to recognize that a value can be named using different units. For example, 45.3 may represent four tens, five ones, and three-tenths, or forty-five ones and three-tenths, or four hundred fifty-three-tenths.

Look Fors

As students work through these activities, check for the following understandings:

✔ Students verbalize the decimal fraction correctly.

✔ Students are able to state the value of a specific digit within a decimal fraction.

✔ Students can construct more than one visual representation for a decimal number.

Coin Values

Complete the chart below for each coin.

Coin	Value $0.00	Representation (10 × 10 grid has a value of $1.00)	Ranking Least, Middle, Greatest

On the back, explain how you decided on your ranking. Also, show the **sum of all three values** and **the difference between any two values**.

Number and Operations: *Foundational Ideas for Representing Decimals*

Name _____ Date _____

Dinner for $10.00

Your mission is to plan a meal without spending more than $10.00. Use restaurant menus to choose your meal.

In the space below, show the following:

- What you bought

- How much you spent for each item

- The total amount you spent

- How much money you have left

Name _____ Date _____

Pathways

Materials • Game board; marker for each player (up to three players); spinner (see Appendix C); and bank (including both bills and coins)

All players begin in the center at $\boxed{\textbf{Start}}$. Taking turns, each player spins the spinner and moves his or her marker in the direction indicated. The player must correctly name the amount of money to stay on the space. If read correctly, the player collects that amount of money from the bank. If read incorrectly, the player does not collect the new amount to add to the total. Play continues until one player reaches a score of $10.00.

$0.89	$6.45	$0.39	$7.09	$2.50
$1.11	$3.00	$5.43	$0.99	$0.01
$6.54	$2.12	**Start**	$0.75	$1.07
$1.23	$1.99	$0.00	$2.33	$0.30
$4.44	$0.07	$8.11	$0.79	$4.08

Patterns

 Misconception

Overgeneralization that all patterns repeat. For example, when given a sequence of numbers that requires an understanding of growth, students repeat the sequence rather than increase it (extending 1, 3, 5, 7,… as 1, 3, 5, 7, 1, 3, 5, 7, and so on, rather than as 1, 3, 5, 7, 9, 11, 13, and so on, which increases by 2 each time).

What to Do

- As the study of patterns begins, be sure to make students aware that there are patterns that repeat as well as patterns that grow. Use cubes, links, square tiles, and other manipulatives to show challenging repeating patterns that students can identify, extend, and then create their own.

- Show students sequences such as: 3, 6, 9, 12, ____, ____, ____, ____, 27, 30, and ask them to fill in the blanks.

- Present students with materials they see every day and ask them to look for patterns within these things.

- Use a calendar and a hundreds chart (beginning with zero or beginning with one) to give students multiple opportunities to look for patterns.

- Expose students to patterns that appear in nature and within their environment.

- Introduce games and activities that require students to use patterns in order to complete the task or win the game.

Look Fors

As students work through these activities, check for the following understandings:

✔ Are students able to identify the growth between numbers?

✔ Are students able to point out patterns that appear in their environment?

✔ Are students able to represent with words, drawings, or symbols the patterns that they identify?

Name _____ Date _____

The Jellybean Problem

Read the problem below. Then use words, pictures, or numbers to figure out the answer. (You may use counters.)

Julio got 1 jellybean on Sunday, 2 jellybeans on Monday, and 3 jellybeans on Tuesday. Figure out how many jellybeans Julio will have at the end of the week.

Algebra, Patterns, and Functions: *Patterns*

Name _____ Date _____

Complete the Patterns

Use crayons to complete these patterns.

Red	Blue	Red	Blue	Red				

Green	Red	Blue	Green	Red	Blue			

Green	Green	Blue	Green	Green	Blue	Green		

Write numbers to complete each of these patterns.

3, 4, 5, 6, ____, ____, ____, 10, 11

12, 11, 10, 9, ____, ____, ____, 5, 4, ____

2, 4, 6, 8, ____, ____, ____, 16, 18, 20

6, 7, 8, ____, ____, 11, 12, ____, ____, 15

Patterns to Extend

Use square tiles to complete these growing patterns. Draw your answers on the back.

a   b   c   d

May be copied for classroom use. © 2010 by Honi J. Bamberger and Karren Schultz-Ferrell from *Activities to Undo Math Misconceptions, PreK–Grade 2* (Heinemann: Portsmouth, NH).

Equals Sign and Equality

⊜ Misconception

Interpreting the equals sign as an operator symbol. Many students interpret the equals sign to mean that an operation must be performed on the numbers to the left and that the result of this operation is recorded on the right of the equals sign. They often ignore the equals sign when presented with nontraditional equations. For example, when given 4 = ___ – 3, students record 1 (thinking 4 – 3 = 1). Many students also may view equations such as 7 = 11 – 4, 3 + 1 = 2 + 2, and 5 = 2 + 3 as incorrect.

What to Do

- Provide multiple part-whole experiences to strengthen number sense. For example, students shake and spill nine bicolored counters and list all resulting combinations such as 9 and 0, 8 and 1, 7 and 2, 6 and 3, 5 and 4, and so on.

- Allow students to represent two-digit numbers in a variety of ways using connecting cubes. For example, 34 is represented as 3 sticks of 10 and 4 single cubes, 2 sticks and 14 singles, 1 stick and 24 singles, and 34 single cubes.

- Provide pairs of students with a two-pan balance and weighted teddy bear counters to explore equality. (These counters can be purchased from most mathematics supply catalogs.) The bear counters come in three sizes (papa, mama, and baby), three proportional weights (12, 8, and 4 grams), and four colors (red, green, blue, and yellow). For example, 1 mama bear is equal in weight to 2 baby bears, or 1M = 2B. Also, 1P = 1M + 1B or 1P = 3B (see page 44).

- Provide opportunities for students to explore with a number balance. This manipulative helps students develop an understanding of equality and inequality, number comparisons, addition, and subtraction.

- Provide students experiences in which they create equivalent representations using Cuisenaire® Rods. An example would be to have students find different ways to represent the orange rod from the set, assigning a value of 10 to this rod. For example, 10 white rods are as long as 1 orange rod.

- Let students explore unknowns in equations by placing number squares to make an equation true (see page 46).

- Ask "Is This True?" regularly and present equations that are recorded in nontraditional ways. For example, 7 = 2 + 5 or 11 + 3 = 20 – 6. Expect students to support their answer with an explanation.

Look Fors

As students work through these activities, check for the following understandings:

✔ Are students able to represent numbers in different ways?

✔ Are students able to demonstrate a variety of representations of different numbers?

✔ Are students able to represent equations in a variety of nontraditional ways?

Name _____   Date _____

Teddy Bear Equality (page 1)

Use the two-pan balance and teddy bear counters to complete the following tasks.

How many different ways can you equal the papa bear?

Use the balance to help find as many ways as possible.

Different colors of bears count as different ways!

For example:

1 blue papa bear = 3 blue baby bears

Algebra, Patterns, and Functions: *Equals Sign and Equality*

Name _____ Date _____

Teddy Bear Equality (page 2)

What would happen if there were 2 papa bears?

How would the numbers change?

List examples below:

Will these equations balance or be equal? Use the two-pan balance to check.

Answer yes or no.

2P = 2M + 2B   _____

3M = 4B + 1P   _____

1B + 1P = 2M   _____

3B + 1M = 1P + 1M   _____

Try your own equations! Record them on the back and ask a friend to complete them.

Mystery Number Squares

Cut apart the number squares at the bottom of the page. Place the number squares in the boxes so each equation is true. Use each number square only once.

☐ = ☐ + 4

8 - ☐ = ☐ + 3

☐ = ☐ + 4

0   1   2   3   4   5

Algebra, Patterns, and Functions: *Equals Sign and Equality*

Foundational Ideas for Functions

 ## Misconception

Students sometimes recognize a relationship between two steps in a growing pattern and assume they have identified the functional relationship. For example, when given a function table, students identify a specific relationship between two terms and apply the same rule to all terms.

What to Do

■ Provide opportunities for students to explore growing patterns. Growing patterns are precursors to functional relationships (in a functional relationship, any step can be determined by the step number, without calculating all the steps in between). Students observe the step-by-step progression of a recursive pattern and continue the sequence.

■ Choose a meaningful context for functional relationships (see page 48). Examples include:

• Money spent on candy

• Ingredients needed for a recipe

• Blocks linked to build towers

• Time required for a relay race

■ Allow students to construct physical models of functional relationships using tiles, toothpicks, connecting cubes, or other hands-on materials. The act of placing toothpicks in a specified pattern or connecting cubes in a sequence can provide insight into the relationship between the two variables.

■ Compare physical models with pictorial or symbolic representations. For example, consider the growing pattern of triangles in "Making Triangles" (see page 49).

■ Model the language of the dependent relationship and encourage students to describe the relationship. Examples include:

• *The amount of money I spend depends on how much candy I buy.*

• *The number of cups of flour needed is determined by the number of pancakes we would like to make.*

• *The height of the tower is affected by the number of blocks linked.*

• *The time required to complete the race is a function of the distance of the race.*

■ Reinforce number sense through estimation. When students are able to articulate their intuitive understanding of the relationship, they may estimate and solve the function simultaneously. Estimation may also help a student more readily recognize an error.

Look Fors

As students work through these activities, check for the following understandings:

✔ Students test their rule for the pattern among many terms to confirm their rule is correct.

✔ Students are able to describe a rule verbally as well as pictorially.

✔ Students can extend increasing and decreasing patterns.

Name _____ Date _____

If ... Then

Complete each sentence with words or pictures.

If one  has 2 wheels, then 2 bikes would have...

If one  has 4 legs, then 3 horses would have...

If I spend $3  on one toy, then _____ toys would cost...

Making Triangles

Use the toothpicks to build the triangles and complete the table.

Triangles	1	2	3	4	5	6	
Picture	△	△▽	△▽△	△▽△▽			
Number of Toothpicks	3 toothpicks	5 toothpicks	7 toothpicks				

How many toothpicks would you need to make 10 triangles? Show how you know.

Name _____ Date _____

More or Less

Complete each sentence using the word *more* or the word *less*.

1. If I buy more candy, I will spend _____ money.

2. If I make fewer pancakes, I would use _____ pancake mix.

3. The faster I work, the _____ toys I can put away.

4. It will take me _____ time if I run faster.

5. The taller my tower, the_____ blocks I will need.

Now you write a sentence using the words *more* or *less*.

Algebra, Patterns, and Functions: Foundational Ideas for Functions

Variables

 Misconception

A lack of understanding about place value and computation yields an inability to use a variable as a digit in an equation.

What to Do

■ Have students identify the elements in a repeating pattern with letters of the alphabet as well as with other descriptors. A pattern made with alternating circles and squares can be called an AB pattern just as easily as it can be named by the shapes within it or the colors of these shapes. This process should be done intentionally to introduce students to the way that letters can be used in mathematics.

■ Have students look for places where a letter is used to represent some word. "Mathematical Equations" can be created in which students replace the letter with the word that makes the equation "true" (see page 53).

■ Point out how letters are used in formulas that are being learned. For example, before students learn formulas to determine the area and perimeter of polygons, they should know the words that these letters replace. If a good problem is given for students to solve, then not only is there a context for the word but the letter replacing it makes even more sense.

■ Begin replacing the "box" in an arithmetic equation with a letter as soon as students recognize the difference between letters and numerals. Start with simple equations and use colored connecting cubes to aid in finding solutions. Most second graders realize that n stands for "number," so equations such as this are no more difficult to solve than if there were a box:

$$n + 6 = 9 \qquad 7 - n = 4$$
$$8 = 5 + n \qquad 5 = n - 2$$

Ask first graders questions such as, "What are all of the possible right answers for this equation: $K + R = 8$." Working together with counters, students can find replacement values for each addend in the equation above. And once students realize that variables can have different meanings, they are less likely to be stumped by a problem that asks them to replace each letter with a digit.

Look Fors

As students work through these activities, check for the following understandings:

✔ Students aren't just looking at the digits and the sign and then following the sign. Be sure they are trying to make sense of the open expression.

✔ Students are using a letter to label things that might have been assigned a numeral (length of a rectangle).

✔ Students can use a number balance to determine the missing addend or sum (see page 52).

Using a Number Balance to Solve Problems

Be sure to look at the entire problem and set it up on the number balance so that the equals sign is your fulcrum. Then solve for the missing number and draw the weights on the number balance below.

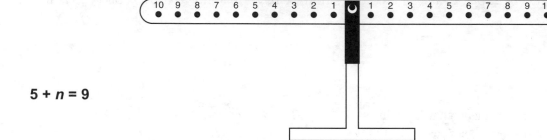

$5 + n = 9$

$8 = 3 + n$

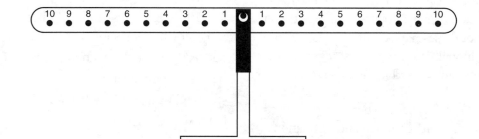

$7 + 5 = n$

$3 + 2 + 4 = n$

Algebra, Patterns, and Functions: *Variables*

Name _____ Date _____

The Mystery of the Missing WORDS

Use the clues to figure out the word that each letter represents. Then write the word in the space.
EXAMPLE: 24 = H. in a D. ANSWER: 24 = Hours in a Day

1. 7 = D. in a W. _____

2. 10 = F. on your H. _____

3. 12 = I. on a R. _____

4. 2 = E. on your F. _____

5. 50 = S. in the U.S. _____

6. 7 = C. in the R. _____

7. 12 = M. in the Y. _____

8. 88 = K. on a P. _____

9. 3 = C. on a T.L. _____

Answers: 7 = days in a week, 10 = fingers on your hands, 12 = inches on a ruler, 2 = eyes on your face, 50 = states in the United States, 7 = colors in the rainbow, 12 = months in the year, 88 = keys on a piano, 3 = colors on a traffic light

Creating Patterns Using Letters

Use the letters below to create your own pattern and then draw your pattern.

EXAMPLE: ABC

AB

AAB

ABB

ABC

Algebra, Patterns, and Functions: *Variables*

Algebraic Representation

Misconception

Teachers sometimes use representations to show students how to understand a mathematics concept, rather than using representations to show how a student is thinking about a mathematical situation. For example, teachers may incorrectly assume that when students use manipulatives, doing so "teaches" them the concept. It is critical to ask students to explain their representation.

What to Do

- Provide opportunities for students to explore, and then talk about, a variety of manipulatives. Model the correct vocabulary that is specific to each manipulative. Plan lessons in which students use these manipulatives.

- Encourage students' use of multiple representations. Create and model an environment in which all explanations and representations are honored and respected.

- Allow students to freely select from different representations to use in solving any problem. Initially, model conventional ways of representing mathematical situations. However, it is critical that students choose and use representations that are meaningful to them (NCTM 2000*). Knowing which type of representation is useful in which situation is an important milestone in mathematical understanding and reasoning for students.

- Ask students to explain and show how they are thinking about a problem during and following a problem-solving task. If students are having difficulty, support them by the types of questions you ask. And, when students hear how others use representations to show how they are thinking about a mathematical idea, it helps them to consider other perspectives. Communicating their thinking requires students to reflect on their problem solving and reasoning; listening to students' explanations enables teachers to determine what students know and can do at any point in time.

- Provide opportunities for students to solve many open-ended tasks with a representation they have chosen. Follow these problem-solving tasks with classroom discussions. Model for students how to record their way of solving a problem using numbers. Be sure to record the students' method both horizontally and vertically.

- Observe when students use a representation to determine if they understand the representation and how to use it to effectively solve the problem. The representation does not show the mathematics to students; rather it models what students understand about the mathematical situation (NCTM 2000*).

- Use literature to engage students in problem solving and ask them to represent their solutions in a representation that makes sense to them (see page 57).

*National Council of Teachers of Mathematics. 2000. *Principals and Standards for School Mathematics.* Reston, VA: NCTM.

Look Fors

As students work through these activities, check for the following understandings:

✔ Students' flexibility in their use of representations to show their thinking.

✔ Student use of appropriate vocabulary in describing a strategy or representation.

Algebraic Representation

Bibliography

Use literature to engage students in problem solving and ask them to show their solutions in a representation that makes sense to them. Following are some examples of literature that promotes open-ended problem solving:

Andreasen, Dan. 2007. *The Baker's Dozen: A Counting Book*. New York: Henry Holt.

> This story describes the sweets a baker prepares before his shop opens. He begins with 1 éclair, 2 cakes, and all the way up to 12 cupcakes. Once the story has been read, ask students to figure out how many total sweets have been baked and to show how they know in a representation.

Carle, Eric. 1972. *Rooster's Off to See the World*. New York: Aladdin.

> On a venture to see the world, a rooster is joined by two cats, then three frogs, then four turtles, and finally five fish. Once the story has been read, ask students to figure out how many total animals there are and to show how they know in a representation.

Giganti, Paul, Jr. 1988. *How Many Snails? A Counting Book*. New York: Greenwillow Books.

> A delightful book that asks a series of questions for students to use visual analysis to determine and count the number of objects on illustrated pages, which are similar yet different. Model for students how to use symbolic representations when they share counting results. This experience helps students develop their understanding of representations using arithmetic expressions.

Merriam, Eve. 1993. *12 Ways to Get To 11*. New York: Aladdin.

> In this engaging book, 12 different ways to get to 11 are demonstrated on illustrated pages. Ask students to represent the different ways (for example, 3 turtles, 2 frogs, 1 lily pond, and 5 dragonflies). The different ways support children in symbolic representation. Challenge children to find all the different ways to get to 13!

Nagda, Ann Whitehead, and Cindy Bickel. 2000. *Tiger Math*. New York: Henry Holt.

> The growth of a Siberian tiger cub is chronicled with a series of different types of graphs that demonstrate the progress of his growth. These graph representations can serve as a springboard for interpreting mathematical relationships in many forms.

How Many Toes?

How many toes are at your work table?

Show your work.

Show a different way to solve this.

Representations of 5

Draw 5 flowers.
Color some flowers red.
Color some flowers yellow.
Tell a friend about your flowers.

Draw and color 5 flowers in a different way.
Color some flowers red.
Color some flowers yellow.
Tell a friend about these flowers.

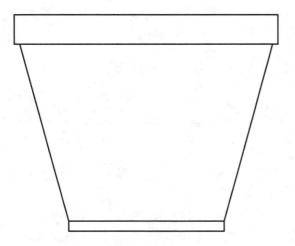

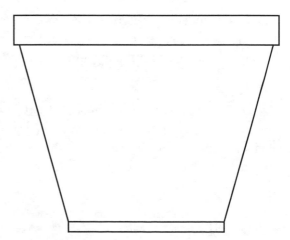

Two-Dimensional Figures

Misconception

Categorizing two-dimensional shapes incorrectly due to overgeneralizing from incorrect examples or the orientation of the shape.

What to Do

- Go on a shape hunt and have students identify shapes in their classroom, school, and home environment.

- Combine geometry with number concepts by having students find different shapes on activity pages.

- Select math-related literature that shows children accurate plane figures.

- Develop some "best examples" ("clear cases demonstrating the variation of the concept's attributes" [Tennyson, Youngers, and Suebsonthi 1983, 281*]) for each of the two- and three-dimensional shapes included in your curriculum since textbooks and posters don't always have these. Ask students questions about these examples to determine whether they recognize the important properties of each.

- Encourage students to describe, draw, model, identify, and classify shapes as well as predict what the results would be for combining and decomposing these.

- Take care in selecting posters, math-related literature, and other commercial displays. Often these items include inaccurate examples of shapes (show rectangles with only two long and two short sides) or incorrect shapes (ellipses that are labeled "ovals" and rhombuses that are labeled "diamonds").

- Allow students to create shapes from a variety of materials so they see regular as well as irregular shapes.

- Play games like "Guess My Shape," where clues are given, students draw a shape after each clue, and then determine the shape being described after all the clues have been read.

- Incorporate other areas of geometry into activities with shapes (for example, creating tessellations and transforming shapes through rotations, translations, and reflections, as well as combining shapes) to give students opportunities to spend more time manipulating and exploring with plane figures.

Look Fors

As students work through these activities, check for the following understandings:

- ✔ Are students able to classify shapes in a variety of ways?

- ✔ Can students name shapes regardless of their position?

- ✔ Can students create both regular and irregular polygons?

*Tennyson, R. D., J. Youngers, and S. Suebonthi. 1983. "Concept Learning of Children Using Instructional Presenting Forms for Prototype Formation and Classification-Skill Development." *Journal of Education Psychology* 75:280–91.

Spy Glasses for Scavenger Hunts

You might want to enlarge the four spy glasses found on this page. Print these on cardstock and then cut out the shape in the center before laminating each spy glass. When students go looking for circles (around the room or school) have them use the circular spy glass. Do the same thing for rectangular, square, and triangular figures. Remember to have students return to the room and draw a picture of the shape they saw and where it was seen.

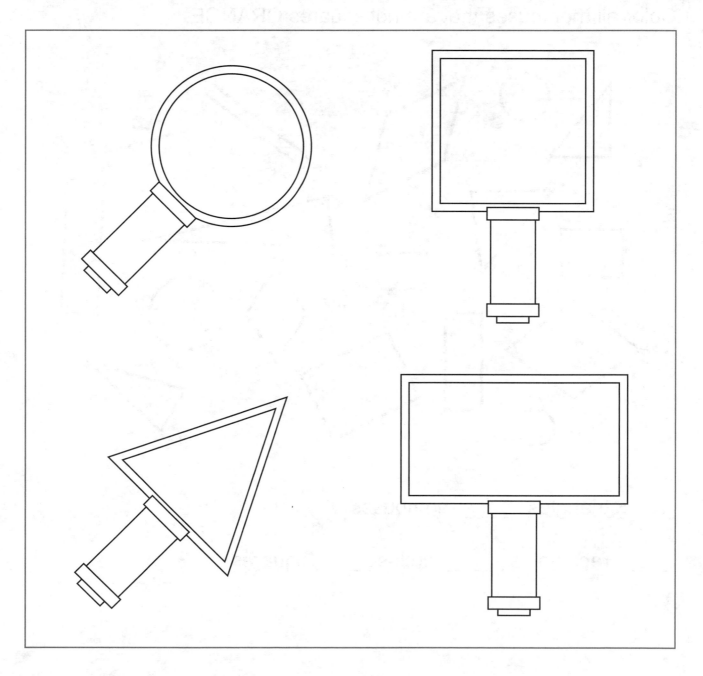

Find the Shapes

Color all rectangles that are not squares RED.
Color all circles BLUE.
Color all triangles GREEN.
Color all squares YELLOW.
Color all rhombuses that are not squares ORANGE.

_____ triangles _____ rhombuses

_____ rectangles _____ circles _____ squares

Name _____ Date _____

Using a Geoboard to Create Polygons

First use a geoboard to create the shapes below. Then draw each shape on these geoboards.

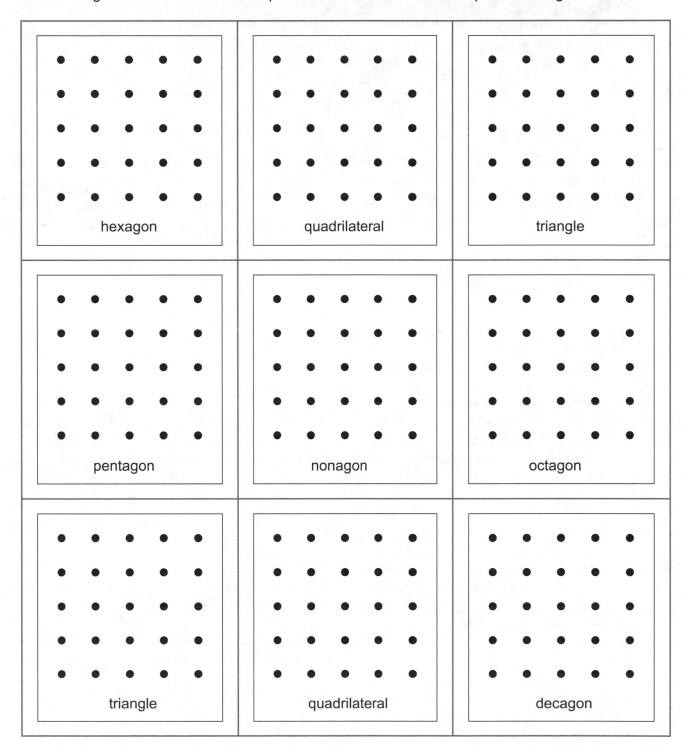

Three-Dimensional Figures

 ## Misconception

Calling a three-dimensional figure by the name of one of its faces. For example, students may call a cube a square.

What to Do

■ Early in the year ask students to look at the building blocks, table blocks, parquetry blocks, and pattern blocks and name them correctly. Use sentence strips to label cubes, cones, cylinders, spheres, and rectangular prisms that appear around the classroom. These words should also be placed on a mathematics word wall, along with photographs and illustrations of each figure.

■ Offer students a range of activities in which they find, color, name, and discuss the solid figures they need to learn. This enables them to generalize the characteristics of a solid figure so that size, color, and other unimportant attributes aren't confusing. Ask questions such as, "Is it OK for this to be a cone even though it's smaller than this cone?" "Can this still be a cylinder even though it's red?" "Would this still be called a sphere even if it was made out of plastic?"

■ Ask students open-ended questions about solid figures so that they can use mathematics vocabulary associated with attributes of these figures. "What can you tell me about this shape?" is a preferred question to "Where do you see a square on this shape?" Eventually, appropriate terminology can be introduced.

■ Have students use "nets" to fold into three-dimensional figures. This allows them to see the faces of the shape prior to its becoming a three-dimensional object (see page 65). Reproducing

the nets on cardstock makes them easier to cut and fold into solid figures.

■ Place solid figures inside a bag and have students feel inside. Without looking, they should name the shape they are feeling. This helps them focus on the characteristics felt and not seen, which could eliminate the distractions of color, size, and or the name of the solids' faces.

■ Provide students with a row of figures (five, for example) where only two are exactly the same and the rest vary in some way. This builds students' visual discrimination and helps them to focus on the concept of alike and different (see page 69).

■ Look for songs on mathematics websites that relate the names of solid figures to attributes that make up each shape. Try: http://mathmadness.org/, http://mathsongs.com/, http:www.songsforteaching.com/Math.html, www.edutunes.com.

Look Fors

As students work through these activities, check for the following understandings:

✔ Are students able to describe and classify geometric solids in a variety of ways?

✔ Can students name geometric solids regardless of their position?

Name _____ Date _____

Guess Which Shape I'll Become

Before cutting out and folding each of the "nets" on the following pages guess which shape each will become. Write this name and how you know this on the paper. Then cut out the "net," fold it on the lines, and see if you are correct.

I think **Figure A** is a _____.

I know this is right because

_____

_____.

I think **Figure B** is a _____.

I know this is right because

_____

_____.

I think **Figure C** is a _____.

I know this is right because

_____

_____.

Figure A

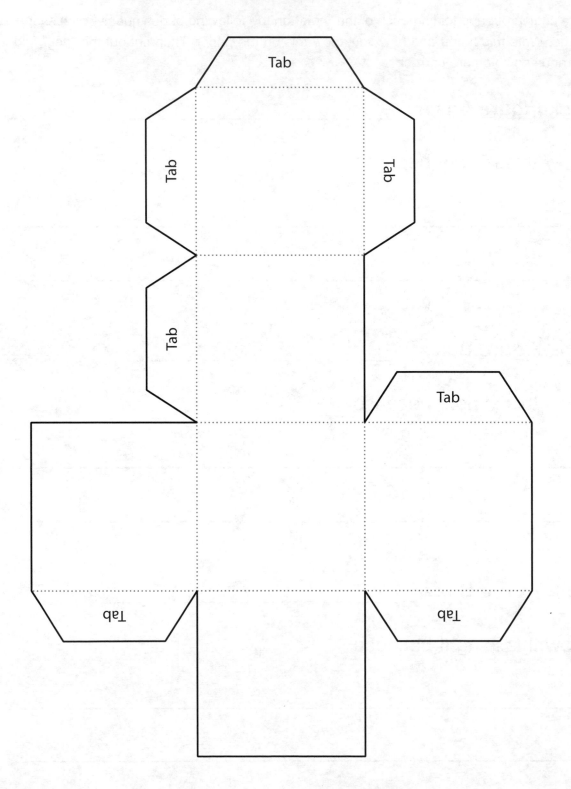

Figure B

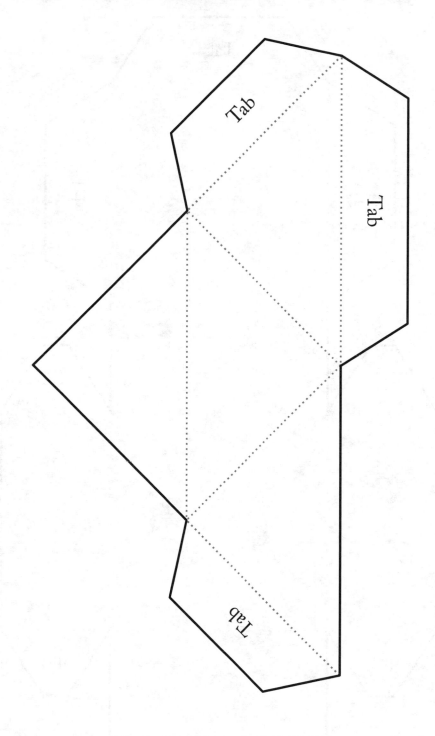

Tab

Tab

Tab

Figure C

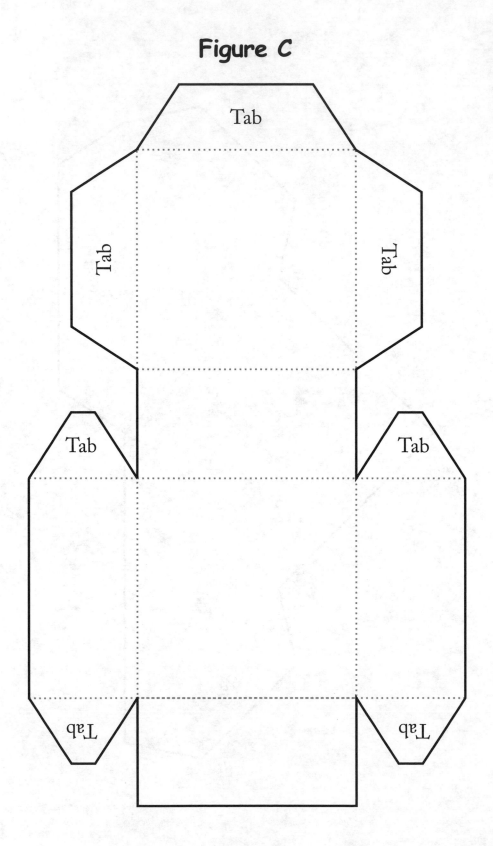

Name _____   Date _____

One of These Things Is Like the Other

Look at each of the pictures and decide which one is like the first one. Put a loop around the one that is just like the first.

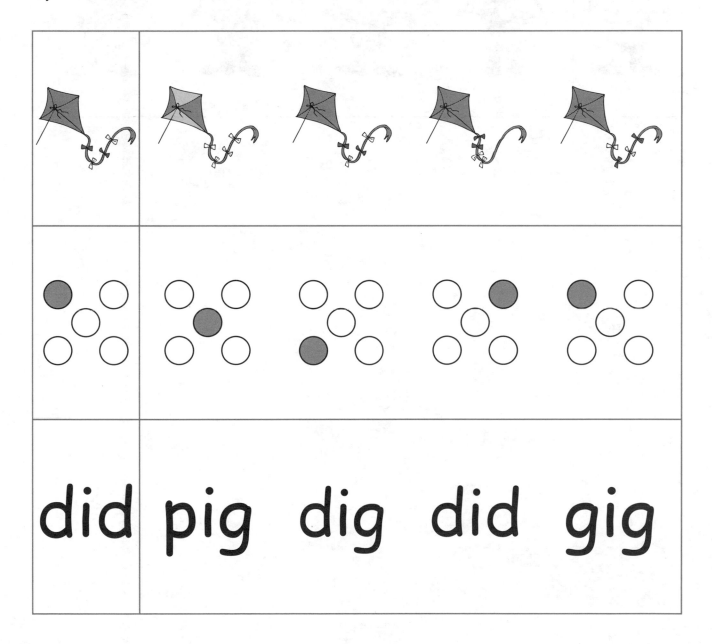

May be copied for classroom use. © 2010 by Honi J. Bamberger and Karren Schultz-Ferrell from *Activities to Undo Math Misconceptions, PreK–Grade 2* (Heinemann: Portsmouth, NH).

Foundational Ideas for Coordinate Geometry

 Misconception

Incorrectly naming points or spaces on a coordinate grid.

What to Do

■ Encourage students to articulate descriptions of location, direction, and distance related to current or future positions. Generate a list of vocabulary words for each of the three categories, such as

- Location: *over, under, behind, between, above, below*

- Direction: *left, right, up, down, north, south, east, west, diagonal, clockwise*

- Distance: *near, far, long, short, inches, miles*

Create a series of steps using these words, and allow students to act them out in order to reach a specific destination. As students generate directions for others to follow, they become aware of the importance of direction and distance when seeking a location (see page 73).

■ With a small group, construct a grid with a large piece of graph paper. Let each student choose a unique game piece to place on the grid. Students should name their location and respond to such questions as:

- How would you describe your location compared to mine?

- How far are you from the origin?

- Which is the shortest path for you to reach another student?

- Do you share a coordinate with anyone else?

■ Provide activities for students to plot points and spaces and to distinguish between the two. The game "Where's Blazer?" requires students to plot points (see page 74). However, when playing such commercial games as Connect Four™ and Battleship™, students name spaces. It is important for students to have experiences with both.

■ Make connections to real-world applications using stories and maps.

- Include students in the planning of an upcoming field trip. Use maps to find the destination, plan the direction needed to travel, determine the distance using the scale, and calculate the approximate time of arrival.

- Allow students to plan a scavenger hunt. Let them draw maps and provide clues for each stop along the path of the final treasure.

- Use a city street map (grid) to explore the notion that there could be multiple ways to get from one place to another, all being the same distance.

■ Anticipate tracking difficulties and make tools available for students as needed. Pipe cleaners work well. One is used as a placeholder for the vertical line segment and a second is used for the horizontal line segment. The point of intersection is the desired point.

Look Fors

As students work through these activities, check for the following understandings:

✔ Are students able to correctly identify the coordinates for a specific space or point?

✔ When given the coordinates, can students identify the specific space or point?

✔ Can students navigate the coordinate grid by following descriptions for a specific location, distance, and direction?

Name _____   Date _____

Which Way? How Far?

■ Choose a starting point and ending point for your partner.

■ Give directions from start to finish:

   • Tell direction: *left*, *right*, *straight ahead*, *back,* and so on

   • Tell distance: number of steps

■ Let your partner know when he or she reaches the final destination.

■ Now your partner can give the directions for you to follow.

Where's Blazer?

Cut out the picture of Blazer below and place him at any point on the grid. Name his location. Describe the moves needed to get Blazer back home, naming each point along the way.

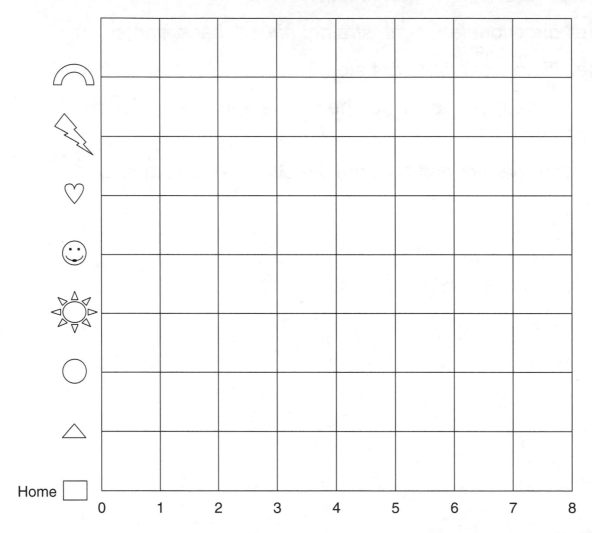

Home

Project the game board and play as a class to guess the predetermined hiding place for Blazer. Allow students to name points, and provide directional clues based on each guess.

Geometry: *Foundational Ideas for Coordinate Geometry*

May be copied for classroom use. © 2010 by Honi J. Bamberger and Karren Schultz-Ferrell from *Activities to Undo Math Misconceptions, PreK–Grade 2* (Heinemann: Portsmouth, NH).

Name _____ Date _____

Four in a Row

Each player uses a different color crayon. Take turns naming the coordinates of a space. If the other players agree the space is named correctly, the player may color the space. The object of the game is to be the first to color four spaces in a row, as shown below.

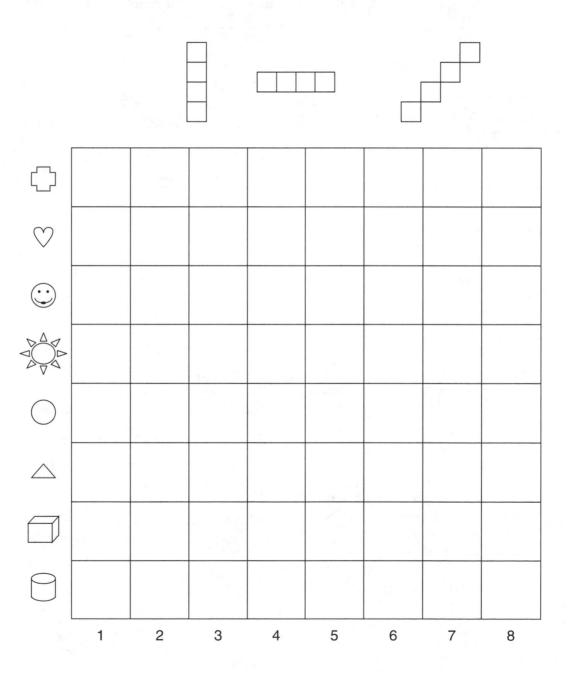

Transformations, Symmetry, and Congruence

▢ Misconception

Due to limited concrete experiences in working with transformations, students overgeneralize that if an arrangement looks different, it must be different and therefore not congruent.

What to Do

- Allow students to role-play flips, slides, and turns with their bodies. For example, ask students to sit on the floor with legs crossed and *slide* backward.

- Provide students with pattern blocks, attribute blocks, or tangram puzzles. They will naturally use transformations to create designs. Ask them to explain how a design was made to reinforce vocabulary such as *flip*, *slide*, and *turn*.

- Find all possible different arrangements for five connected squares (see page 77).

- Allow students to investigate transformations on the computer. The National Council of Teachers of Mathematics has links to a variety of programs on the Illuminations website. Kid Pix is another option.

- Show examples and nonexamples of symmetrical designs and pictures.

- Model how to place a mirror perpendicular to a design or picture to show a symmetrical reflection. Place several mirrors in a center area with a variety of pictures so students can further explore symmetry.

- Provide pattern blocks for making a design on one side of a fold in a sheet of paper. Once the design is created, ask students to trace around each block in the design. Partners then exchange papers and recreate a reflected design on the other side of fold.

- Present vertical lines of symmetry first (when students are modeling with, for example, pattern blocks). Later, provide opportunities for students to explore horizontal lines of symmetry.

- Provide paper-folding experiences that turn into artwork. Students fold a sheet of paper in half, apply paint in dabs on half of paper, refold, and then unfold the paper to reveal a symmetrical design. Students could also fold a piece of paper in half, cut out the design on the fold, and then open it to reveal a symmetrical design.

- Provide geoboards for students to create symmetrical designs or pictures.

Look Fors

As students work through these activities, check for the following understandings:

- ✔ Are students able to describe and model transformations accurately?

- ✔ Are students able to recognize, model, and describe symmetry and congruence?

Five Squares: How Many Arrangements Are Possible?

For this investigation, students will find all possible arrangements for five squares. Students use visualization and spatial-reasoning skills when they apply transformations: slides (translations), flips (reflections), and turns (rotations).

You will need the following materials:

■ 1″ color tiles, 1 bucket per 4 students

■ 1″-square grid paper, 2 or 3 per student

■ scissors, 1 per student

■ crayons or markers

Explain that there are rules to follow when making their arrangements:

■ Each square tile must have at least one whole side touching another

This is OK. ▭▭▭▭▭   This is not OK. ⌐⊓⊓⌐

■ Each arrangement must be different

■ Sliding, flipping, and turning are required when checking whether a new arrangement is different.

Ask a volunteer to arrange two color tiles on an overhead projector. This figure, called a *domino*, has only one possible arrangement. If students say there are two different arrangements, show how to rotate arrangement to show they are the same. Repeat with three color tiles (which is called a *triomino* and has two possible arrangements). Finally, students arrange four color tiles (called a *tetromino* and having five possible arrangements). When students are familiar with the expectations of the investigation, challenge them to find all the different possible arrangements for five squares (a *pentomino*).

Distribute color tiles, grid paper, and markers. Students use color tiles to first explore the possible arrangements. Explain that each time they find an arrangement that is different, they should record it on grid paper. When arrangements are cut out, students can slide, flip, or turn them to check whether arrangements have already been made. It is recommended that students work in small groups to complete this investigation.

Allow students to explain their strategies in determining that all possible different arrangements were found. Some students may notice that arrangements resemble letters of the alphabet and may use this as a way to check their arrangements. It is recommended that you not tell students there are twelve arrangements possible.

Note: A more detailed lesson with a student dialogue is described in *Introduction to Reasoning and Proof, Grades 3–5* by K. Schultz-Ferrell, B. Hammond, and J. Robles (The Math Process Standards Series, S. O'Connell, Series Ed. Portsmouth, NH: Heinemann, 2007).

May be copied for classroom use. © 2010 by Honi J. Bamberger and Karren Schultz-Ferrell from *Activities to Undo Math Misconceptions, PreK–Grade 2* (Heinemann: Portsmouth, NH).

Name _____ Date _____

Five Squares: How Many Arrangements Are Possible?

Five Squares: How Many Arrangements Are Possible?

(Reference Sheet for Teacher)

Spatial Problem Solving

 Misconception

Inability to create mental images of objects.

What to Do

- Provide visualization opportunities for students to develop their "mind's eye" (see page 82).

- Allow students to manipulate and build using a variety of materials, such as multilink cubes, wooden blocks, and connecting cubes. These tactile experiences provide opportunities to view different transformations of figures. Ask students to describe their movements and end products. This is also an opportune time to develop vocabulary as the terms relate to the students' specific work.

- Present small groups of students with several nets and geometric solids. Challenge the students to match each net to its corresponding solid. Allow students to confirm their predictions by cutting and folding the nets to form solids. Additionally, instruct students to trace each face of a solid to form their own nets. They may then cut out their nets and fold to form solids.

- Place a geometric solid on the overhead projector to show the shape of one face for students to see (conceal the solid using a file folder standing up on end at the end of the projector between the class and the geometric solid). Continue manipulating the solid to project each face. Ask the students to name the solid. This activity helps students make a connection between the shapes of the faces and the three-dimensional solid the faces form.

- Let students make two-dimensional representations of three-dimensional figures using Cartesian graph paper or isometric graph paper (available free online).

- Provide puzzles for students to complete using tangrams, pattern blocks, pentominoes, and Geo-Reflectors™.

- Present students with sets of cards showing the top, front, and side view of a figure made with connecting cubes. Students then construct the figures using the visual clues.

- Look for geometric shapes and figures in works of art. Some suggestions include: *The Traveler* by Liubov Popova, *Composition with Red, Blue, and Yellow* by Piet Mondian, and *Brooklyn Bridge* by Joseph Stella.

Look Fors

As students work through these activities, check for the following understandings:

✔ Can students describe shapes and figures and relate them to real-world objects?

✔ Are students able to match two-dimensional representations with the corresponding three-dimensional objects?

Draw What You Saw

Choose one of the images below and transfer it to a projector. Flash the image for students to see for just a few seconds. Instruct students to draw what they saw. Finally, show the image again so students can compare their representations to the original. Repeat the process with another image. Use images that are familiar to students or resemble something familiar so they are able to make a connection to something they see often.

Geometry: *Spatial Problem Solving*

Name _____ Date _____

Try, Try Again!

Gather 4 blue rhombuses from the pattern block bucket. How many *different* shapes can you make with 4 rhombuses? Build your shapes in the boxes below.

View and Build

Use blocks or connecting cubes to build the figures below.

#1	#2
#3	#4
#5	#6

Geometry: *Spatial Problem Solving*

Telling Time on an Analog Clock

 ## Misconception

The hour hand and minute hand are confused, or the student names the numeral closest to the hour hand regardless of whether this is appropriate. For example, when given the time of 2:45 on an analog clock, students say that it's 2:09, 9:02, forty-five minutes past three, or ten minutes past nine.

What to Do

■ Begin instruction knowing that young children need to learn two things about time: the passage of time, and how to tell time. Have students share things they do at different times of the day, using words and illustrations.

■ Introduce the telling of time by using an hour-hand-only clock. Have students make observations about this device and play "Complete the Clock" so they begin an awareness of the placement of the numerals around an analog clock face (see page 86).

■ Use index cards, colored sticky dots, and paper fasteners to create a clearer understanding of the five-minute intervals around an analog clock face (see page 88).

Look Fors

As students work through these activities, check for the following understandings:

✔ Can students correctly place the numerals around a clock face?

✔ Can students discuss the fractional distance between numerals when an hour hand is positioned between one numeral and another?

✔ Are students able to count by fives and demonstrate an understanding of the relationship between the numeral on the clock face and the number of minutes past the hour?

✔ Can students articulate the relationship between the part of the hour that has passed and the numeral on the clock that is being pointed to?

Name _____ Date _____

Complete the Clock

See Appendix D for the clock to be used with this activity.

Toss 2 dot cubes. Figure out the total amount of dots.

Place the number that represents this total in the correct circle of the clock.

Keep tossing the 2 cubes until every small circle has a number in it except for the *1*.

When only the *1* is left you may use only 1 die.

Keep tossing until you get a 1 and can complete the clock.

Measurement: *Telling Time on an Analog Clock*

Half Past the Hour

Look at each clock and write what time you see based on the hour hand.

It is _____.

It is _____.

It is _____.

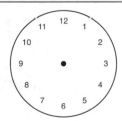

It is _____.

Read the times given and draw the hour hand in the correct place.

It is half past three.

It is half past six.

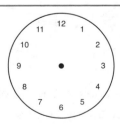

It is half past eight.

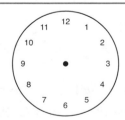

It is half past eleven.

Making a Clock

You will need 12 white index cards (5″ × 7″); 12 yellow, pink, blue, or green index cards (3″ × 5″); 4 different colored sticky dots (15 of each color); paper fasteners; and a hole punch.

To prepare for this activity, take 15 of 1 color sticky dot and place 5 on the long side of each of 3 white index cards (see Figure 1). Then do the same with the other 3 colors of sticky dots, placing 5 on the long side of each of 3 white index cards. Punch 2 holes in the corner of each card (see Figure 2). Use paper fasteners to attach all of the cards so your clock is connected in a circle. Once the clock is assembled write the numerals 1–12 on the colored index cards and place these around the clock (see Figure 3).

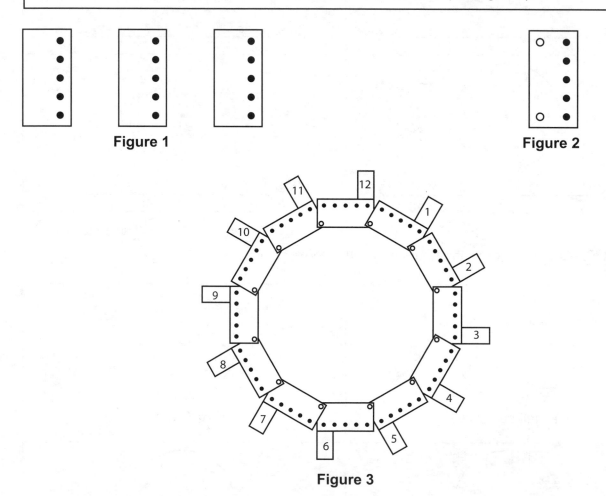

Figure 1

Figure 2

Figure 3

To begin, ask for 12 volunteers to come forward and stand in line—one next to the other. Have each student hold up 1 hand with their 5 fingers spread apart. Ask, "How many fingers do you think your friends are holding up? What could we do to figure this out?" Take their ideas, but encourage them to use counting by fives to get their answer.

Measurement: *Telling Time on an Analog Clock*

Once they have counted by fives, starting with 5, ask them which person would say, "15." Ask them to share how they know this and what it means. Say, "If I am counting by fives and I stop on 45, which person in our line would I be stopping at?" Do this for several other examples. Then give each student in the line one of the colored numeral cards (to show their place in the line). Ask the class how these students could be arranged so that they looked more like a clock than a number line. Have students arrange themselves into a circle and be sure that the 12 is opposite the 6 and the 3 and 9 are across from each other.

Tell students that between each numeral on an analog clock there are 5 minutes. Say, "Today we are going to count around the clock in 5-minute *intervals*." Show them the word *interval* and add it to the word wall, letting them know that it means "the space between things." Have each student with a numeral count by fives (beginning with 1), while another student walks from 12 to 1, from 1 to 2, from 2 to 3, and so on. Ask students if they remember how many minutes have passed when the walking student arrived at the 6. Have a different student do this again and stop at the 6. The class will be on 30 and this is when you reveal to them that the student has walked halfway around the clock. Ask, "So, how many minutes is half of an hour?"

Lay the index card clock on the floor and have students place their numerals around it. Have students talk about the different colors of sticky dots and what this might mean. With a circle split into fourths, colored in the same color as the sticky dots, show the relationship between the fourths of the circle and the fourths of the floor clock. Ask questions about what part of an hour has passed if 15 minutes have passed, 30 minutes have passed, and 45 minutes have passed.

Determining the Value of Coins

 ## Misconception

Overgeneralizing the value of coins when counting them; for example, students count coins as individual objects or equate a coin's size to its value.

What to Do

- Provide opportunities for students to observe and describe attributes of coins. Give each student a magnifying lens to more closely examine these coins. Create coin webs to record students' descriptions of attributes noticed.

- Use real coins.

- Use children's literature to pose problem-solving questions that support students' understanding of 5, 10, and 25 (see page 92).

- Skip-count by 5s, 10s, and 25s. Use real coins to help facilitate skip counting.

- Tape a penny onto a connecting cube, a nickel onto five connected cubes, a dime onto two sticks of five cubes, and a quarter onto five sticks of five cubes. Students concretely and visually see the number of "ones" in 1, 5, 10, and 25.

- Provide sets of coins for students to count that are only a nickel and some pennies or a dime and some pennies. Later, include a quarter and some pennies. When students are ready, add more than one nickel with some pennies, and so on.

- Play "10 Dimes" (see page 94).

- When counting money, use only two types of coins initially, and give a signal when a shift occurs. For example, display three dimes and two nickels, point to the coins with the greatest value first (dimes) and ask students to count (10¢, 20¢, 30¢). Hold up your hand to indicate a pause and then bring your hand down. Point to the coins with the smaller value (nickels) and continue to count (35¢, 40¢). Pausing between counts signals a different type of counting will occur next (Van de Walle and Lovin 2006, 151*).

- Provide hundreds charts for students to visually and concretely see the amount of pennies in nickels, dimes, and quarters (Drum and Petty 1999, 264–68*).

- Provide opportunities for students to place coin amounts in order according to values. Give partners a bag of real coins (pennies, nickels, dimes, and quarters) and ask them to take turns rolling a dot cube and taking that number of pennies. They exchange coins only when it is their turn. The game continues until a partner trades for a quarter.

*Van de Walle, J., and L. Lovin. 2006. *Teaching Student-Centered Mathematics: Grades K–3*. Boston: Pearson Education.
*Drum, R., and W. Petty, Jr. 1999. "Teaching the Value of Coins." *Teaching Children Mathematics*. Reston, VA: NCTM.

Look Fors

As students work through these activities, check for the following understandings:

✔ Are students able to organize coin sets before determining the value?

✔ Can students trade five pennies for a nickel, two nickels for a dime, and so on?

Determining the Value of Coins

Bibliography

Use literature to engage students in problem solving and counting money. Following are some examples of literature that promote open-ended problem solving in authentic situations:

Brisson, Pat. 1995. *Benny's Pennies*. Edmond, OK: Dragonfly Books.

> This book motivates young children (prekindergarten and kindergarten) to think about combinations that make up five pennies. Benny has five pennies to spend on presents for his family. Display different types of stickers with prices of 1¢, 2¢, 3¢, 4¢, or 5¢ (for example, a student may say he could buy three stickers: 1¢ sticker, 2¢ sticker, and another 2¢ sticker.)

Glass, Julie. 2000. *A Dollar for Penny*. New York: Random House.

> Penny sells lemonade and collects three quarters, one dime, two nickels, and five pennies to make one dollar. Engage students in investigating other combinations of coins that make one dollar.

Maccarone, Grace. 1998. *Monster Money*. New York: Cartwheel Books.

> This book engages students in exploring all the possible coin combinations for a dime. The Monster Pet Store is selling pets for 10¢. Each pet is purchased with a variety of coin combinations. Allow students to represent a monster pet of their choosing and a combination of coins to pay for it.

Murphy, Stuart J. 1998. *The Penny Pot*. New York: HarperCollins.

> The children in this story are paying 50¢ to go to the face-painting booth. Provide time for students to explore the different coin combinations for 50¢.

Nagel, Karen B. 1996. *The Lunch Line*. New York: Scholastic.

> Kim forgets her lunch at home and needs to buy lunch in the cafeteria with the coins she finds in her pockets: two quarters and five dimes. Ask students to examine the cafeteria menu and think of different ways Kim could have spent her money.

Rocklin, Joanne. 1995. *How Much Is That Guinea Pig in the Window?* New York: Scholastic.

> A class has $50 to buy a classroom pet and explore different pets along with the cost of taking care of them. Students reinforce computations skills as they follow along with the story.

Slater, Teddy. 1998. *Max's Money*. New York: Scholastic.

> Max is saving money to buy his mother a present. This book contains suggestions for how to enhance students' money concepts and skills. It is recommended for grades 2 and up. For example, a game is explained in which students reach into a paper bag to "feel" the coins needed to make an amount designated by the teacher.

Name _____ Date _____

How Many in a Dollar?

Copy three sheets per student. On the first page, students should circle a group of five 1¢ boxes to equal each nickel. The process is repeated for determining the number of dimes and then the number of quarters in a dollar.

A nickel is worth 5¢. How many nickels are in a dollar? _____

A dime is worth 10¢. How many dimes are in a dollar? _____

A quarter is worth 25¢. How many quarters are in a dollar? _____

1¢	1¢	1¢	1¢	1¢	1¢	1¢	1¢	1¢	1¢
1¢	1¢	1¢	1¢	1¢	1¢	1¢	1¢	1¢	1¢
1¢	1¢	1¢	1¢	1¢	1¢	1¢	1¢	1¢	1¢
1¢	1¢	1¢	1¢	1¢	1¢	1¢	1¢	1¢	1¢
1¢	1¢	1¢	1¢	1¢	1¢	1¢	1¢	1¢	1¢
1¢	1¢	1¢	1¢	1¢	1¢	1¢	1¢	1¢	1¢
1¢	1¢	1¢	1¢	1¢	1¢	1¢	1¢	1¢	1¢
1¢	1¢	1¢	1¢	1¢	1¢	1¢	1¢	1¢	1¢
1¢	1¢	1¢	1¢	1¢	1¢	1¢	1¢	1¢	1¢
1¢	1¢	1¢	1¢	1¢	1¢	1¢	1¢	1¢	1¢

Name _____   Date _____

10 Dimes

Taking turns, each player rolls 2 dot cubes, names the total amount of dots showing, and places that many pennies on his mat. When 10 pennies are accumulated, they are exchanged for a dime, which is placed on the dime side of the mat. The game continues until one player has 10 dimes.

10 Dimes	
Dimes	**Pennies**

Measurement: *Determining the Value of Coins*

Units versus Numbers

 Misconception

Viewing the process of measuring as a procedural counting task. For example, students count the markings on a ruler (rather than the units), resulting in an incorrect measurement of length.

What to Do

- Provide multiple opportunities for students to describe the attributes of a variety of objects and identify what could be measured on each to find their size.

- Allow students to compare objects and expect them to describe the results. This task reinforces vocabulary specific to measurement, such as *longer*, *shorter*, *wide*, and *narrow*.

- Ask students to sort a variety of objects into groups based on a designated object, such as a marker. Students sort objects into three groups: objects shorter than the marker, longer than the marker, and about the same length as the marker.

- Ask students to estimate the size of an object first before measuring it. Expect students to explain why they think their estimate is reasonable.

- Allow students to measure real-world objects. This exercise forces children to approximate measure, a more realistic application of measurement.

- Encourage students to measure the same object with a variety of nonstandard units and units in a variety of sizes.

- Bridge nonstandard units to standard units by providing manipulatives that are "standard" size (such as one-inch color tiles, one-centimeter cubes, Cuisenaire® Rods, base-ten blocks).

- Allow students to make their own rulers to help them understand that it's not just a tool used to complete a procedural task (see page 97). Students' focus will be on the one-inch spaces, or units. Engage students in comparing student-made rulers to standard rulers.

- Initially, provide students with rulers with only inch markings to help students understand that each space (instead of a mark) on a ruler represents a unit. Then provide half-inch rulers. Students will be better prepared to use traditional rulers, which are filled with markings that are confusing to them!

- Use rulers with the "0" mark a short distance from the edge. Students will be engaged in thinking about both endpoints when measuring with this type of ruler. They will also be focusing on units (and not markings) when they measure.

Look Fors

As students work through these activities, check for the following understandings:

✔ Do students understand that when units are small, more are needed to measure, and when units are larger, fewer units are needed?

✔ Can students explain why they think their estimates are reasonable?

✔ Can students explain what numbers mean on a standard ruler or the starting point on each ruler?

Length Scavenger Hunt

Grab a handful of connecting cubes.
Connect them together to make a stick.
Use this stick of cubes to measure.

My "stick" has _____ cubes.

A _____ is longer than my stick.

A _____ is shorter than my stick.

A _____ is about the same length as my stick.

Put your objects in order.
Start with the shortest object.
Draw pictures on the back of this paper to show how you ordered your objects.

Measurement: *Units versus Numbers*

Name _____ Date _____

Measurement

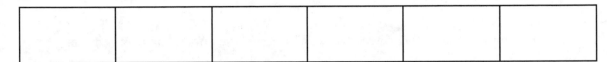

Unit Ruler

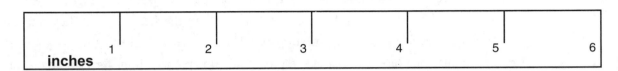

Inch Ruler

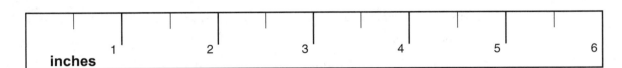

Half-Inch Ruler

Units versus Numbers

Bibliography

Hightower, Susan. 1997. *Twelve Snails to One Lizard*. New York: Simon & Schuster.

This book focuses informally on the following units of measure: twelve inches in a foot, thirty-six inches in a yard, and three feet in a yard. It is recommended to be used only as an introduction to the standard units of inch, foot, and yard. After reading the story, provide each student a twelve-inch strip of adding machine tape (plain with no markings). Ask them to look around the classroom to find objects that are about the same length. They can record what object they found on their strip of paper. Then give each student a thirty-six-inch strip of adding machine tape and repeat the process. At this point, a hunt for this length can be done outside the classroom. This exercise familiarizes students with benchmarks of one foot and one yard even though they are not formally using the standard tools.

Lionni, Leo. 1995. *Inch by Inch*. New York: HarperCollins.

Students use inch rulers (see page 97). Prepare a measuring chart for students to record the results for the following:

• First, ask students to name an object in the classroom that is about one inch in length (without measuring). They record their predictions on a recording sheet and then measure the object to verify the prediction. Finally, they list additional objects that are about one inch in length.

• Students repeat this process by predicting an object in the classroom that is about three inches, record their predictions, and measure the object to verify. They record additional objects that are about three inches.

• Finally, ask students to predict what object in the classroom is about six inches, record their predictions, and again measure the object to verify. They record additional objects that are about six inches.

Pinczes, Elinor J. 2001. *Inchworm and a Half*. Boston: Houghton-Mifflin.

It is recommended this book be read and used when students have an understanding of half-inch units on a ruler and an understanding of the fractions ½, ⅓, and ¼. Students use half-inch rulers (see page 97) to measure a variety of objects. Prior to completing this task, choose objects that are six inches or less for students to measure. Also, choose several objects that are slightly longer than six inches. Ask students to think about how these objects can be measured and to represent how it was done.

Area and Perimeter

 Misconception

Confusing the terms *area* and *perimeter*.

What to Do

■ Allow students to explore area by covering the surface of a variety of objects with nonstandard units (for example, covering the top of a table with foam cutouts or covering the outline of a student's hand with a collection of rocks) (see page 100). This exercise helps them see area as the amount of surface within specific boundaries. Then move on to covering surfaces using congruent units, such as index cards or multilink cubes. Using a consistent unit allows students to compare the areas of different shapes.

■ Have students compare the area and perimeter of two different figures using the same units.

■ Connect the concepts of area and perimeter to meaningful scenarios like those in children's books. *Spaghetti and Meatballs for All!*, by Marilyn Burns, is a great story for promoting discussion. It explores how the arrangement of the same number of tables (area) impacts the amount of available seating (perimeter). Make connections to science by planning a school garden. Allow students to determine how to get the greatest area given the allotted space.

■ Give students a set amount of squares and triangles (pattern blocks work well) to use to make a design. Compare the varying designs created. Compare the area of each. Discuss the notion of conservation of area. Get students to recognize that although the designs vary in appearance, the area is consistent for all.

■ Have students use pattern blocks or square tiles to create a variety of designs with a constant perimeter. Instruct students to compare the areas of the shapes made with like materials. Discuss what trends they notice about the area of shapes that all have the same perimeter.

■ Provide cutouts of rectangles, triangles, trapezoids, and circles and have students develop strategies to compare the area of each. They may cut the pieces in order to overlap and decide which is bigger.

■ Let students walk around the edge of a carpet to estimate the perimeter. Allow students to cover the carpet to estimate the area (using students as the units).

Look Fors

As students work through these activities, check for the following understandings:

✔ Do students understand that the distance around the perimeter of a figure is different from the amount of space covered by a figure?

✔ Can students cover a figure with units and count the number of units used?

✔ Are students able to see that the size of the units affects the number of units needed to measure the area or perimeter of a figure?

Footprints

Trace your footprint. Use counters to fill the space.

I used _____ counters to cover the area of my footprint.

Measurement: *Area and Perimeter*

Name _____ Date _____

Which Pizza Is Bigger?

Use chips, beans, or cubes to find the bigger pizza.

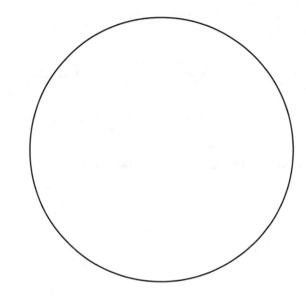

Measurement: *Area and Perimeter*

Name _____ Date _____

Making Shapes!

1. Use modeling clay to make different shapes, such as the ones shown below.

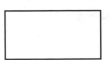

2. Cut a piece of string to show the distance around the outside of each shape.

3. Put the strings in order from shortest to longest.

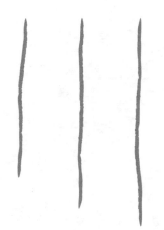

Measurement: *Area and Perimeter*

Foundational Ideas for Conversions

 ## Misconception

When adding or subtracting with different units of measure students rename with units of ten or regroup with units of ten (just as you do when you rename or regroup with whole numbers). For example, applying what they know about *tens* when renaming inches to feet or minutes to hours.

What to Do

- Give students time to explore with whatever units of measure are being used, prior to giving students problems to solve (whether they be story problems or numerical expressions).

- Have students record different ways to represent the same unit of measure (see page 104).

- Have students discuss what they might have to do if they want to know what the difference would be between two units of measure when subtracting involves renaming. (For example: What if you had 2 hours before your bedtime. You watch a television program and 2 commercials and see that 37 minutes have passed. How will you figure out exactly how much time you have left to stay up?) Ask students to share their ideas for solving a story problem like this and then discuss whether these answers make sense.

Look Fors

As students work through these activities, check for the following understandings:

- ✔ Look to see that students represent addition and subtraction of time, length, or fractions with the appropriate conversions.

- ✔ Have students use illustrations, whenever possible, to represent different ways to name the same thing.

- ✔ Provide students with manipulative materials to represent fractions in multiple ways.

The Same Answer Shown in Different Ways

Use a centimeter ruler to figure out the length of the following lines. Be sure to show this in both centimeters and millimeters.

_____   _____ cm _____ mm

_____   _____ cm _____ mm

_____   _____ cm _____ mm

_____   _____ cm _____ mm

Use a calculator to figure out different ways to show these amounts of time. Remember that there are 60 seconds in a minute and 60 minutes in an hour.

3 hours   _____ minutes   _____ seconds

2½ hours   _____ minutes   _____ seconds

5 hours   _____ minutes   _____ seconds

3½ hours   _____ minutes   _____ seconds

Measurement: *Foundational Ideas for Conversions*

Name _____ Date _____

Showing Money in Different Ways

1. A fruit juice from the vending machine costs $.75. You have lots of nickels, dimes, and quarters. Show *4 different ways* you could buy this juice.

2. A bag of cookies from this same machine costs $1.25. You can use only coins (no bills) to get these cookies. Show *4 different ways* you can buy these cookies.

3. If you buy both the juice and the cookies, how much money will you have spent? Show what you did to figure this out.

Honi J. Bamberger and Karren Schultz-Ferrell from *Activities to Undo Math Misconceptions, PreK–Grade 2* (Heinemann: Portsmouth, NH).

Name _____ Date _____

Learning About Liquid Measure

Use real measuring cups, pints, quarts, and gallons to figure out the answers to these problems.

1 gallon is the same as: _____ quarts

_____ pints

_____ cups

2 quarts is the same as: _____ gallons

_____ pints

_____ cups

2 pints is the same as: _____ gallons

_____ quarts

_____ cups

Measurement: *Foundational Ideas for Conversions*

Sorting and Classifying

 ## Misconception

Overgeneralizing the meaning of vocabulary associated with sorting because of limited experiences. For example, when students are asked to sort by "matching," they may choose only one attribute associated with the original sorting rule, such as placing a small yellow circle in a group that has only large circles (because it is a circle but ignoring the size difference).

What to Do

- Involve students in daily cleanup and reorganization of classroom materials. This activity provides ongoing opportunities to sort and match materials.

- Provide experiences for students to identify and describe the attributes of an object. For example, if students are exploring lids ask them to choose a lid to describe. Ask pairs of students to compare their lids, and to tell how they are alike and how they are different.

- Provide a variety of materials for sorting and classifying. Begin with *structured* materials, such as teddy bear counters or pattern blocks, which have easily identifiable characteristics.

- Allow students to work with attribute blocks (see page 109). These tools are designed to develop flexible reasoning, which will support children when they reason about the characteristics of the data.

- Introduce *unstructured* materials gradually because these materials are more difficult to describe and classify. Scaffold the language necessary for students to describe their sorts. Examples of unstructured materials include seashells, buttons, shoes, or students themselves (see page 110).

- Allow students to decide on a sorting rule. This exercise encourages them to use ideas they own and understand. Then expect children to explain how they sorted. Children benefit from hearing others' reasoning for a sorting rule.

- Let students sort collected data and represent them pictorially. Provide time for students to describe how their data were organized. For example, students might draw their favorite lunch food from the cafeteria. As a group, students sort the food pictures into groups and then tell what they notice about the data.

- Support children when they are sorting two- and three-dimensional shapes by encouraging them to describe how the shapes are alike and how they are different. This support helps them build appreciation for definitions of shapes. They will later use these understandings to create classes of shapes (for example, quadrilaterals).

- Connect students' informal language to more formal mathematics language used in organizing, describing, and analyzing data (such as *all*, *some*, *not*, *equal*, *most*, *fewer*, *similar*, *in common*, and *predict*).

Look Fors

As students work through these activities, check for the following understandings:

✔ Can students compare objects and describe how they are alike or different?

✔ Can students state a sorting rule based on the attributes of the objects?

✔ Can students sort a set of objects in two different ways and then describe how the groupings were made?

Using Attribute Blocks

Attribute blocks are considered structured materials because their attributes are easily identified and described by children. These blocks allow children to focus on the reasoning skills necessary to complete tasks. Attribute blocks have four distinct attributes: shape (rectangle, square, triangle, hexagon, and circle), size (large and small), color (red, yellow, and blue), and thickness (thin and thick). Several tasks that support students' abilities to describe attributes, sort, and think logically follow:

- Exploration. Allow students to first explore attribute blocks before completing any tasks. In a whole-group discussion, ask students to tell what they noticed about the blocks when they were exploring them. Record their descriptions on chart paper. For example, if a student says the blocks are different colors, begin a list of the colors for the attribute blocks.

- Comparing Blocks. Ask students to choose their favorite block. In pairs, students describe their blocks to each other, including how they are alike and how they are different.

- How Long Can We Make It? Arrange students in a circle on the floor. Place an attribute block in the center so that all can see it easily. Ask students to describe its attributes. Then place another block next to it that is different in only one way. For example, a thick, large yellow hexagon is placed next to a thin, large yellow hexagon. These blocks are only different in one way: thickness. Challenge students to figure out what block could be next and to state how they know it goes next. A thin, large yellow square could go next, which is different only by shape. Students continue to place blocks until no more blocks can be placed. Students are focusing on attributes and explaining their reasoning in their choice of blocks.

- In or Out? Record a "rule" (for example, "small, thick shapes") on a 5″ × 7″ index card. Arrange students in a circle on the floor. Place a large hoop in the center of the circle. Turn the index card upside down and place it on the hoop. Tell students they will be choosing shapes to place inside the hoop, and that you will respond "in" or "out" based on the mystery rule. After students have chosen about seven shapes, they will begin to notice how the shapes inside the hoop are alike. Ask them to describe this similarity as well as describe the other shapes still outside the hoop. Then ask them to explain their reasoning in choosing shapes they think will go inside the hoop. Finally, ask students to think about what the mystery rule could be and to explain their reasoning for how they know this. Depending on the mystery rule, this task can be easily differentiated. When students are comfortable with this experience, they can create the mystery rule and challenge a partner to name the rule by noticing how shapes are placed inside or outside the hoop.

Button Tasks

Buttons are considered an unstructured sorting material because they have a variety of attributes. Some of the different attributes are: size, shape, number of holes, textures, designs, colors, letters, or types of button material (such as metal, wood, and plastic). Children benefit from the complexities involved in sorting buttons because it reinforces their creativity in deciding how to make groups.

■ Introduction. Read the book, *The Button Box,* by Margarette S. Reid. This book presents a nice introduction to the different attributes of buttons. The book contains illustrations of many types of buttons, which provide students with opportunities to notice and describe their attributes.

■ Exploration and Comparing. Give each student a bag of five buttons (ten buttons for older students) and a work mat. Ask student to first explore their buttons. Pairs of students then describe their buttons to each other. Ask students to choose their favorite button and compare it to their partner's favorite button. How are the two buttons alike? How are they different? Ask students to share their comparisons with the whole group.

■ Sorting. Students need opportunities to notice and describe the many attributes of buttons and then time to compare how buttons are alike or different before they are able to sort them. In initial sorting tasks, limit the number of buttons given to students (for example, a bag of ten buttons for a pair of students). Too many buttons can be overwhelming because of the number of attributes that could be involved. When students have completed their sorting, ask them to explain how they sorted. Then challenge them to re-sort the same buttons in a different way.

■ Attribute Cleanup. A few examples follow of ways to help students place their buttons back into the bag after a task is completed:

• Place the buttons with 4 holes into the bag.

• Place the buttons with no holes (those having a shank) into the bag.

• Place the buttons that are shaped like a circle into the bag.

■ Button Logic. Use the following logic clues with the four buttons on the following page. Students focus on the buttons' attributes to think logically about which buttons to eliminate in order to name the button being described. Before revealing the clues, ask students to describe what they notice about the buttons first.

• There are fewer than 4 holes on the button. Which button could it be? How do you know? (Once students have explained their thinking, place a small sheet of paper over the button with 4 holes.)

- The number of holes on this button is between 1 and 3. Which button could it be? How do you know? (Cover the button with a flower once student have explained their thinking.)

- There are no curved lines on this button. Which button could it be? How do you know?

On another day, change the clues and reuse the button page.

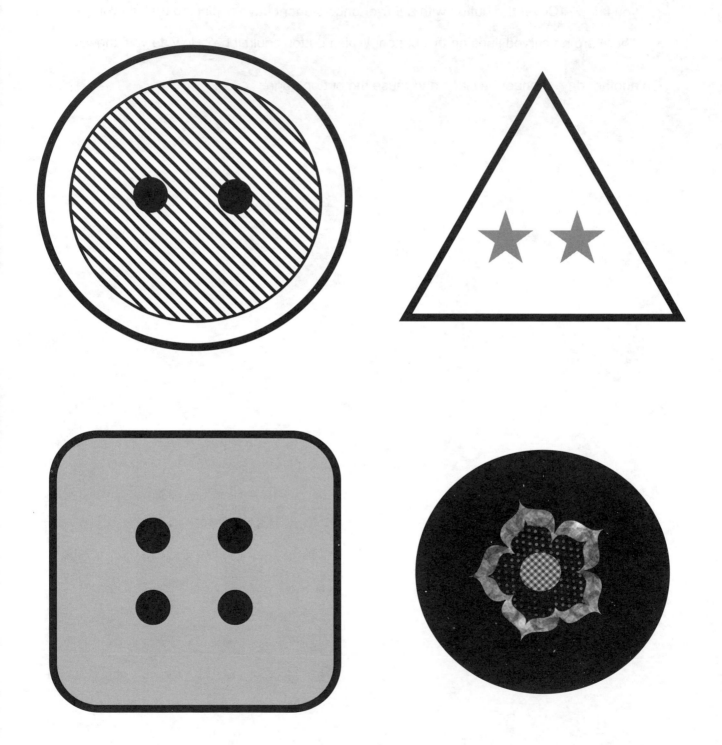

Data Analysis and Probability: *Sorting and Classifying*

Name _____ Date _____

Sorting Storybooks

Decide on a way to sort these books into groups. Describe how you are sorting and then make a list of these books in the groups you have made.

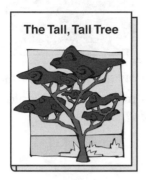

The Tall, Tall Tree
by Anna Cook

Flowers in the Spring
by Jackson Brown

The Happy Caboose
by Laura Smith

Trains All Around Us
by Jared Waters

Springtime Is Fun
by Anna Cook

Animals Found in Africa
by Warren Smith

Cars, Trucks, and Planes
by Meg Cook

Tigers and Lions Roam Free
by Warren Smith

Tulips, Pansies, and Roses
by Pete Nguen

Helicopters Twirl
by Julio Martinez

Wonderful Animals
by Sam Mondo

Flowers and Other Plants
by Jesse Washington

I sorted these books by _____.

Here are my groups:

Data Analysis and Probability: *Sorting and Classifying*

Sorting Solid Figures

For this activity, you will need a variety of wooden solids in the bag, including cones, cubes, spheres, rectangular prisms, cylinders, and pyramids.

Test these shapes to see if they spin, roll, stack, and slide. Use the chart below to write "yes" or "no" for each shape.

	Spin	Roll	Stack	Slide
Cone				
Cube				
Sphere				
Cylinder				
Rectangular prism				
Pyramid				

Now that you have tested these solid figures, decide on a way to use this information in the comparison circles below. Write the label on each circle, and then place the name of the shape that fits into each part of the Venn diagram.

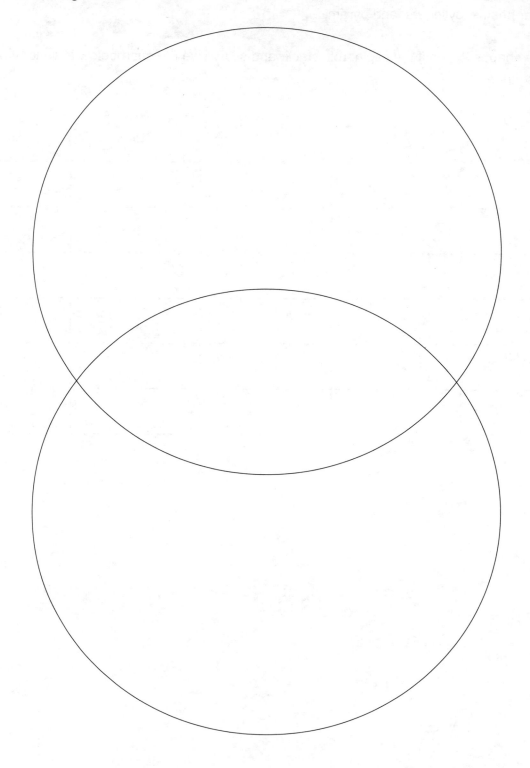

Choosing an Appropriate Display

Misconception

Any type of display can be used for a set of data.

What to Do

■ Make the data collection and analysis process meaningful by helping students first identify the question they wish to answer. Formulating the question provides direction in the collection and representation stages. Rather than graphing favorite ice cream flavors or class birthdays simply for the sake of making a graph, create a purposeful question the graph is meant to answer. Students will learn the parts of a graph and how to put the pieces together, with intent and purpose. Possible questions for elementary students include:

• If we are buying ice cream for an upcoming celebration, which three flavors should we buy?

• How will we know when someone in our class is celebrating a birthday?

• How can we keep track of how everyone gets home from school in the afternoon?

• What types of books should be purchased for the library?

• Where in the room is the best place for our plants to grow?

■ Provide examples of both numerical and categorical data so students will be more likely to understand why certain data displays are more appropriate than others.

• Numerical examples: age, shoe size, height, money earned

• Categorical examples: kinds of pets, movie types, foods, names

■ Ask students to collect graphs from newspapers, magazines, and websites. Sort the examples according to types. Allow students to speculate why a specific graph was used to represent the data and why another representation would not work as well to convey the information.

■ Create two different displays for a given set of data. Ask students to compare the two displays and discuss whether they carry the same message. This activity will help students see that the kind of graph they choose can impact the visual message. (One way to do this is by using connecting cubes to represent the bars on a bar graph. Students can then replicate the quantity of each color and arrange them in a circle to see how the same data would look as a circle graph.)

■ Make large versions of graphs as a class (an easy way is to use a shower curtain liner and traffic tape). These visual aids enhance class discussions about the parts of a graph and the most appropriate way to display the data.

■ Gather a collection of graph templates to which students can refer. These visual prompts can help students compare the potential final product and help connect the data to a potential display.

Look Fors

As students work through these activities, check for the following understandings:

✔ Can students recall the question being answered through the collection and display process?

✔ Do students understand the parts of each type of data display appropriate for their grade level?

✔ Can students compare the attributes of different types of displays?

Name _____ Date _____

Data Matching Is a Picnic

The data below show food served at a picnic. Complete the tally chart to match the data.

Picnic Foods Served

Food Served	Number Served
Hot dogs	
Burgers	
Chicken	

May be copied for classroom use. © 2010 by Honi J. Bamberger and Karren Schultz-Ferrell from *Activities to Undo Math Misconceptions, PreK–Grade 2* (Heinemann: Portsmouth, NH).

Name _____   Date _____

What's the Same? What's Different?

Look at the two bar graphs. Tell a friend how they are alike and how they are different.

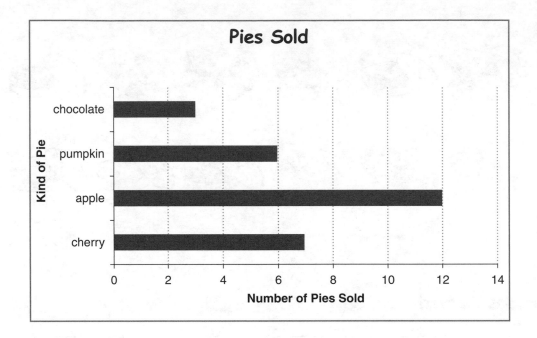

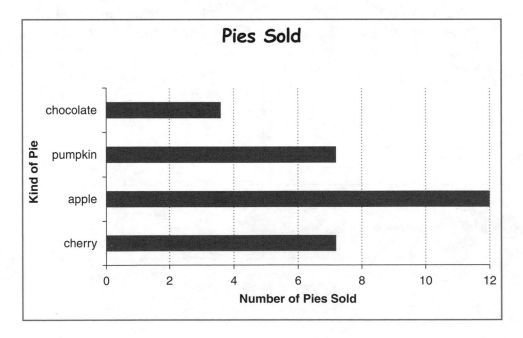

Name _____ Date _____

Collecting and Displaying Data for a Purpose

Which lunch is the favorite at your school? Who might be interested in these data?

1. Use the table below to survey students and find the favorite lunch choice at your school.
2. Use the data to make a bar graph.
3. Share your findings at your school.

Lunch Choice	Tally	Total

Analyzing Data

Misconception

Incorrectly analyzing the data on a graph.

What to Do

■ Use color to distinguish different categories of data on a graph (different-color connecting cubes or links when creating a graph with manipulatives, multicolored crayons or markers when constructing graphs on paper). Color variations allow students to more readily compare and contrast the data.

■ Designate a space in the classroom in which to display a variety of tables and graphs. Encourage students to collect examples as well. Make a daily data chat part of the morning routine. Ask students to share what the data show, and brainstorm who might be interested in such information.

■ Ask students to describe the shape of data—the visual image conveyed by a graph. Provide graphed data minus the titles and labels. Ask students to describe the trend they see and name some possible titles and labels based on those trends. Or conduct this activity as a matching game: titles and labels on one set of cards, graphed data on another. Have students match the data to the correct title and labels.

■ Give students different-size representations of the same data. (Modifications might include changing the scale or the length of the axis.) Ask them to consider what is revealed by the different perspectives. Examples like these prompt rich discussions

of comparisons and visual messages. Helping students realize how choices with regard to the axes and the scales influence the appearance of the data will help learners be more critical in their data analysis.

■ Use technology to expose students to multiple views of the same data. Many software programs and applications allow students to input quantities and then choose from a variety of displays. With the click of the mouse, students can see the data transformed from a bar graph to a circle graph. By comparing the data as represented on different types of graphs, students can decide which provides a clearer picture of their intent. If students choose an incorrect display you can ask about the validity of the data and the appropriateness of the graph given the data set.

Look Fors

As students work through these activities, check for the following understandings:

✔ Can students link the data points to the display to explain why the graph looks the way it does?

✔ Are students able to explain the graph to others?

✔ Can students describe how a graph might change if there were a change in the data?

Sports Watched on TV

			🏈
			🏈
	🏀		🏈
	🏀		🏈
⚽	🏀	⚾	🏈
⚽	🏀	⚾	🏈
⚽	🏀	⚾	🏈
Soccer	**Basketball**	**Baseball**	**Football**

What can you say about the data display?

Data Analysis and Probability: *Analyzing Data*

Name _____ Date _____

How Long Is That Book?

Book Title	Number of Pages
Caps for Sale	
Ten Black Dots	
The Button Box	
Math for All Seasons	

 **equals 10 pages**

Write two observations about the data above:

1.

2.

Name _____ Date _____

True or False?

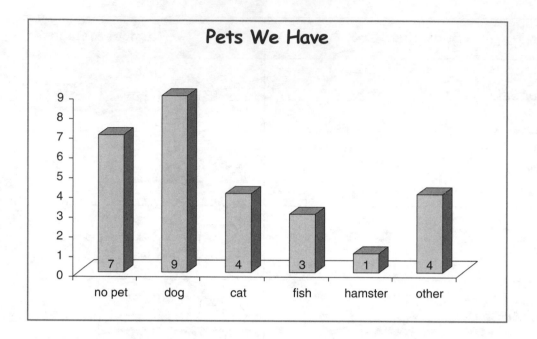

1. Three students have fish for pets.   True *or* False

2. More students have fish than cats. True *or* False

3. Hamsters and dogs equal 10 pets. True *or* False

4. Most students have no pets. True *or* False

Data Analysis and Probability: *Analyzing Data*

Name _____ Date _____

Graph Scavenger Hunt

Search for a graph (newspaper, magazine, Internet) and glue it in the space below. Write the story the graph tells on the back.

Foundational Ideas for What Does "Fair" Mean?

 ## Misconception

Believing that factors other than having an equally likely opportunity to win make a game or activity fair.

What to Do

- Provide spinners split into two halves of different colors and let students spin and record the outcome. Compile data from all students to demonstrate that there is an equally likely chance for both colors to get landed on.

- Use manipulatives that students are familiar with to do experiments (coins, dice, bicolored chips) and record the data to determine the likelihood of an event occurring.

- Have students name the colors of the candies inside "fun-sized" packages, and then open the package to determine whether there are the same amount of each color. On their own students will say that it isn't fair that there are more of one color than another.

- Discuss situations where probability is used in the real world. Weather makes sense to young students who can certainly explain why it is unlikely that it will snow in the summertime or be hot in the middle of the winter. What makes the most sense to them is what children will be wearing during different seasons (depending on where they are from in the country). Activities can be developed that connect science and mathematics as children predict the clothing that will be worn when a spinner lands on each of the seasons.

Look Fors

As students work through these activities, check for the following understandings:

✔ Fairness involves having an equally likely opportunity to be spun, picked, or worn.

✔ Just because an activity is fun does not mean that it is a fair activity.

✔ If there are more of one thing than another, it is likely that the greater amount will make the activity unfair.

Blue, Red or Yellow?

See Appendix E for the spinner to be used with this activity.

Which color will get landed on the most? _____

Keep a tally to show what happens.

BLUE	RED	YELLOW

Which Color Will Be the Most?

Sort your candies by their color.
Write how many you have of each color.

RED   GREEN   YELLOW   ORANGE   PURPLE

Do you think that your bag of candies was fair? Explain your thinking.

_____

_____

_____

What would make the bag fair?

_____

_____

_____

Name _____ Date _____

Which Color Is More Likely to Be Pulled?

Inside your bag there are 5 yellow, 4 red, and 1 green cube. Look inside to be sure.

Close your eyes and take turns pulling out *1* cube. Record the color and then put it back.

When you have had *20 turns*, look at the data that you collected and be ready to talk about what happened and whether you were surprised.

1.   2.   3.   4.

5.   6.   7.   8.

9.   10.   11.   12.

13.   14.   15.   16.

17.   18.   19.   20.

Name _____ Date _____

Is It Certain, Possible, or Impossible?

Read each statement. Decide whether it is certain (will always happen), possible (could happen), or impossible (will never happen). Put a check in the column to show your answer.

	Certain	Possible	Impossible
It will be sunny tomorrow.			
An airplane will be seen in the sky.			
I will watch TV.			
If a coin is flipped it will land on heads.			
I will breathe today.			
Cereal will fall out of the clouds.			
A telephone will ring in my house.			
I will use the computer today.			
Books have pictures or words.			
Scissors cut paper.			
Ice cream will be for dessert today.			
The grass in the park is purple.			

Choose one of the statements and draw a picture to show this.

Appendix A

Spinners for "Spinning for a Sum" Activity (page 10)

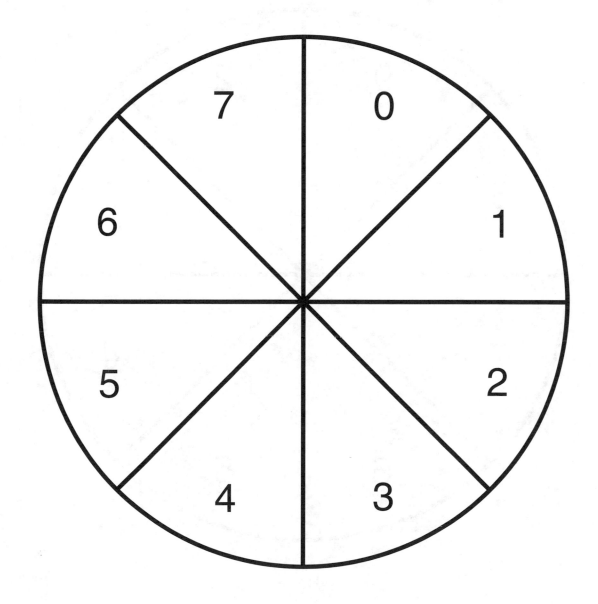

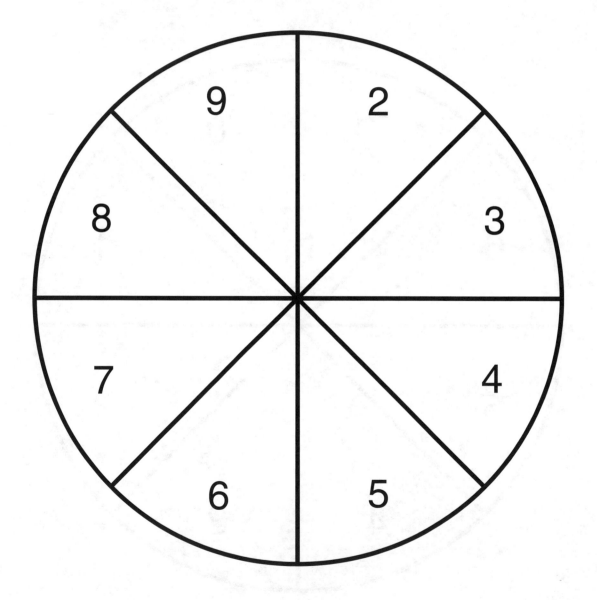

Spinner for "Equal Groupings" Activity (page 19)

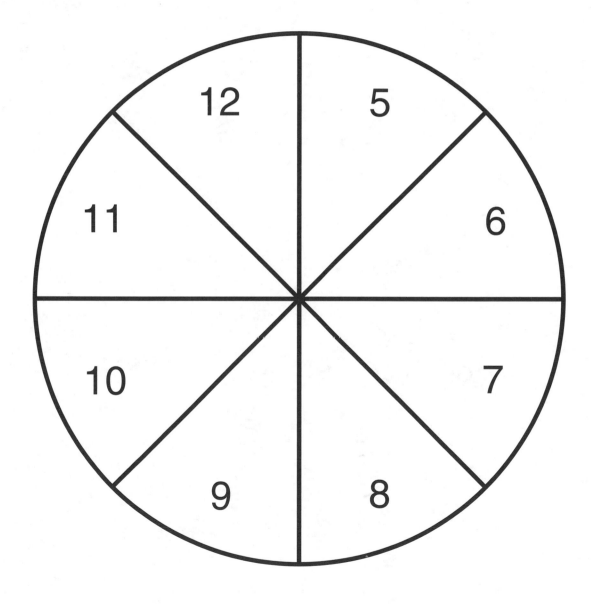

Spinner for "Pathways" Activity (page 38)

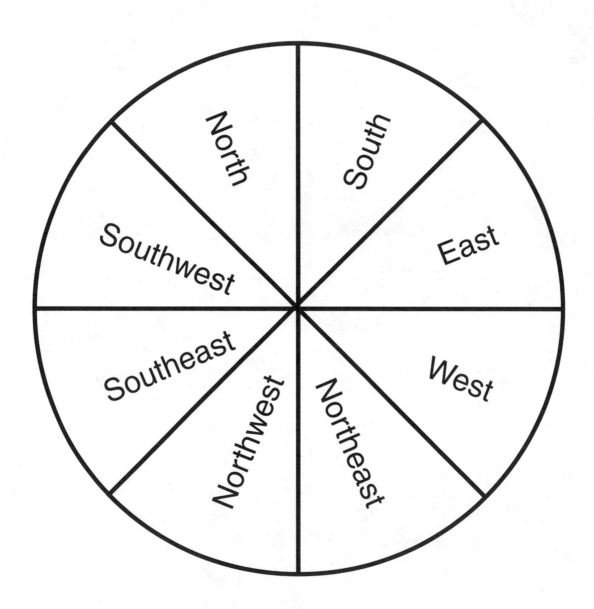

Clock for "Complete the Clock" Activity (page 87)

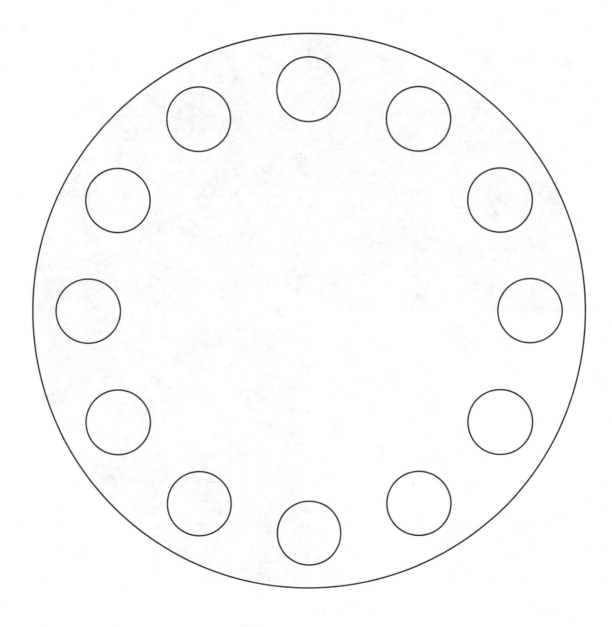

Spinner for "Blue, Red, or Yellow?" Activity (page 129)

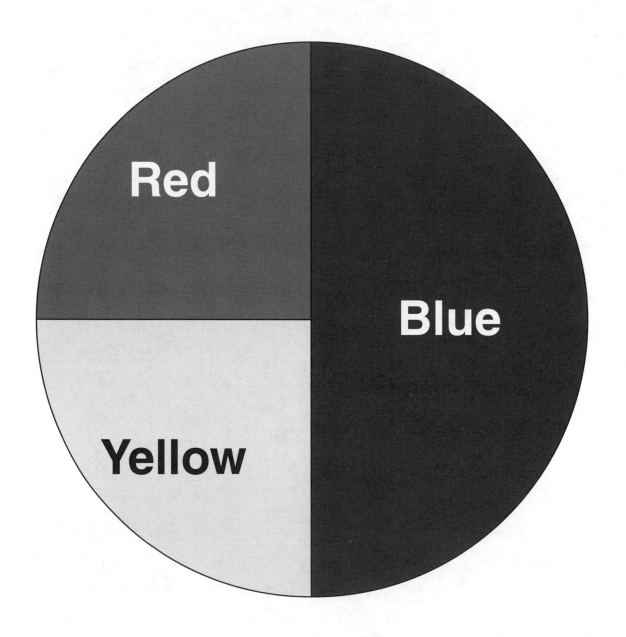